QUICKBOOKS
for RESTAURANTS

A BOOKKEEPING AND ACCOUNTING GUIDE

A MUST-HAVE
QUICKBOOKS GUIDE FOR
RESTAURANT OWNERS
AND OPERATORS

ZACHARY WEINER

THIRD AVENUE
PUBLISHING

Copyright © 2019 by Zachary Weiner

All rights reserved.

No part of this publication may be reproduced, distributed, or transmitted in any
form or by any means, including photocopying, recording, or other electronic
or mechanical methods, without the prior written permission of the publisher,
except in the case of brief quotations embodied in critical reviews and certain other
noncommercial uses permitted by copyright law. For permission requests, write to
the publisher, addressed "Attention: Permissions Coordinator," at the address below.

Third Avenue Publishing LLC
157 E. 86th St. #506
New York, NY, 10028
info@thirdavenuepublishing.com

Limit of Liability/ Disclaimer of Warranty:
While the publisher and author have used their best efforts in preparing this book, they
make no representations or warranties with respect to the accuracy or completeness
of the contents of this book and specifically disclaim any implied warranties of
merchantability or fitness for a particular purpose. No warranty may be created or
extended by sales representatives or written sales materials. Neither the publisher
nor the author shall be liable for any loss of profit or any other commercial damages,
including but not limited to special, incidental, consequential, or other damages.

ISBN-13: 978-0-578-55624-6
ISBN-10: 0-578-55624-3

Ordering Information:
Quantity sales. Special discounts are available on quantity purchases by corporations,
associations, and others. For details, contact the publisher at the address above.

All trademarks and service marks (whether or not registered) are the
property of their respective owners. All company, product and service names
used in this book are for identification and educational purposes only. Use of
these marks does not imply endorsement or affiliation of any kind.

*QuickBooks, QuickBooks Online, QuickBooks Desktop, QuickBooks Enterprise, and
Intuit are trademarks of Intuit Inc., and registered in the U.S. and other countries.
All other trademarks cited herein are the property of their respective owners.*

This book is dedicated to those that dream big
and those that lift them up to dream even bigger.

CONTENTS

1

INTRODUCTION

A HELLO

Running a small business is challenging, confusing, and at times over-whelming. For restaurant owners, this is even more true. Obviously, because you're reading this book, you know that restaurants are simply more challenging than a standard small business. A restaurant is one of the few types of businesses where inventory is literally manufactured daily, in the same facility in which it is sold, and is sold sometimes within seconds of manufacture. There are logistical challenges all over the place, from staffing headaches and production issues, to crazy hours and costs increasing from every possible angle.

Running a restaurant is one of the most challenging positions to be in, and restaurants often have the most limited resources. Having been in the trenches from both an operational and a financial standpoint, I understand the challenges of this business well, know the headaches personally, and will work in the coming chapters to make the day-to-day accounting aspects of your restaurant business a bit easier.

SUCCESS

Every businessperson wants to succeed, regardless of their business. But success is defined differently by different people. In this book, I define success as maintaining true and accurate financials that allow you, the business owner, to make better business decisions resulting in increased profit.

Often times, restaurant owners are 100 percent hospitality focused. That means they live, breathe, and eat customer relations. They are often on the floor nightly, ensuring that operations run smoothly. In these situations, the "back office" can be overlooked, forgotten about, and commonly pushed to the back of the brain. However, I want this book to persuade you that the back office is your friend: Its interests are intimately aligned with your interests. The goal of a back office is to ensure compliance and to help owners and operators better understand their business so they can more efficiently drive profits.

Of course, having your back office in order is just as important as having a great team at your disposal. That is why this book, and a CPA with restaurant expertise, will help drive your business forward toward continued profitability. This book outlines the core principles and concepts to get you on the right track of restaurant accounting success. Because questions or complex issues often come up, however, referring to a qualified CPA will help you address minor issues before they become major issues. QuickBooks should also be a big part of your restaurant's success. It can easily play an integral role in helping you manage items like gift cards, bill payments, and cash flow, as well as more exciting things like profitability. Having an up-to-date accounting system like QuickBooks will also allow you to properly plan and prepare for the coming years. QuickBooks can help you set up budgets, understand the seasonality of your business, and keep a keen eye on cost of goods. These all play a role in the difference between the long-term success or failure of your restaurant.

BIRD'S EYE VIEW

Before discussing the ways that QuickBooks and other accounting systems can help you, I want to start at the top, taking in your entire operation and explaining how everything in your restaurant business comes together.

Most restaurants function the same way: There is a front-of-house department and a back-of-house department. These two core departments are rarely on the same page and usually communicate through a computer system called a point of sale (POS). Your restaurant likely lives and dies by the POS system. The waitstaff enters orders either in a full-service or quick-service capacity; then the chefs or cooks receive that ticket, process it, and prepare the food. The waitstaff or associated runners then take the finished product (the meal) to the guest, provide hospitality to said guest, and move on to the next customer.

Once the day is done, registers are closed out. The accounting work is left for the next morning and tracks not only what happens in the POS system, but also in your back fridge, your daily deposits, your employees' timesheets, and much more. The accounting system brings all these different components together to help you better run your business.

CONCLUSION

Throughout the course of this book, you will learn some of the key setup, features, and systems that will help you go deeper into your business. Most restaurants are not as profitable as they should be, and few business owners and operators know why. In the upcoming chapters, I will walk you through becoming a business owner and operator who understands their pain points and knows how to act on them to drive bottom-line results. By utilizing the forthcoming systems and processes, my goal is to help you drive operational efficiencies, ease of reporting, and profitability

2

THE MANY VERSIONS
OF QUICKBOOKS

CHOOSING THE CORRECT QUICKBOOKS PRODUCT

One of the most challenging pieces of starting a new project or updating a historical system is getting it off the ground. This chapter will help you to quickly get your QuickBooks accounting project started or updated to better serve you. With so many software options, sometimes it can be overwhelming to choose the right one. This chapter clearly outlines the options and their features, with the goal of helping you select the right QuickBooks product for your business. Having used all the products I outline here, I am confident that I have distilled the complexities of each version down into an easily consumable overview to help you best make your purchasing decision.

RESTAURANT SOFTWARE SPECIFICS

The coming chapters will cover how to use the QuickBooks software to best run your restaurant accounting department. That said, the following chapter leaves it to the reader to make the best selection of software based on their preference and budget constraints. The one mistake I often see when owners choose QuickBooks software is a belief that a restaurant needs software with complex inventory accounting features. The good news is that such features aren't necessary, and I cover why in-depth in Chapter 10. So, don't simply upgrade to the most advanced offering because you believe your inventory needs require it.

WHAT THE PEOPLE SAY

People have strong preferences about most things, and the version of QuickBooks they swear by is no exception. Have you ever spoken to your grandparent or parent, and they wistfully mentioned how it used to be? You know, back when they walked up the hill both ways in the snow, all year around? Or when they used to buy a can of Coca Cola for $.15 cents. Ahhh, the good old days.

These are the same people who, in the accounting world, preach that QuickBooks Desktop—the system they live and breathe by—is the best version of QuickBooks. For these people, QuickBooks Online version is just too "weird." Of course, this claim has no real basis in reality. It's just that many people are used to QuickBooks Desktop, and QuickBooks Online feels too new. However, both Intuit products solve basic daily accounting challenges. Deciding which version you want to use will come down to your preferences and needs.

Both the Desktop and Online products are useful. In fact, I will let you in on a little secret: I outline a different way to manage inventory for your restaurant—what I call the quick and dirty way—that does not require QuickBooks inventory features. This means that none of the many levels and versions of QuickBooks really matter. (That is, unless you have an accounting team of 10 and want to set separate permissions for each individually, then I would recommend QuickBooks Enterprise. Unless you run a large multi-unit restaurant group, with an employee specializing in recording sales, another employee focused on accounts payable and a controller managing the innerworkings reporting to your CFO, the permissions and advanced functionality add little value to your business.)

Other than that, you are free to run the gambit of QuickBooks options. If you like working online, then go with QuickBooks Online. If you like working on a desktop, then go with QuickBooks Desktop. If you like being online, but want to use the desktop version, well, use the blended desktop online with a verified Intuit host. In the coming pages, I'll help you decide by outlining the different QuickBooks programs and offering some details about them. The final decision is up to you.

QUICKBOOKS FOR MAC DESKTOP

WHO'S IT FOR?
This is a bit obvious, but this product is for Mac users. With the many keyboard tricks integrated into the Mac operating system, QuickBooks for Mac enables the user to reach optimum efficiency.

WHERE DOES IT LIVE?
The QuickBooks files and applications live on your Mac. The company file can be stored on an external hard drive, but to ensure that you do not corrupt the file, it is best to have this stored on your Mac.

WHAT FEATURES ARE INCLUDED?
All the features you would expect from a desktop version of QuickBooks are included. For an extra fee, the file can be hosted in the cloud, allowing access from multiple Mac computers located at different locations.

WHAT FEATURES ARE FORGOTTEN?
Cloud hosting and automatic updates are not included in the version for Mac desktops. Additionally, you are limited to access by only three users, so it has potential to limit you as you grow your small business.

WHAT'S IT COST?
The real cost of the software is $299 per year, but it also requires an annual support contract of $299 that recurs yearly.

IS IT USER-FRIENDLY?

What is great about the Mac for QuickBooks is that it is built for Macs. QuickBooks for Macs makes use of Mac keyboard shortcuts, and as an avid Mac user myself, I know that keyboard shortcuts save time (and thus money)!

WHAT ELSE DO YOU NEED TO KNOW ABOUT THIS SOFTWARE?

Of all of the desktop versions of QuickBooks, the Mac version is the least robust. As your business grows and you need a more advanced version of QuickBooks, you will be all but forced to move to the PC versions. QuickBooks Pro, QuickBooks Premier, and QuickBooks Enterprise are PC-based systems, so it may be best to focus your energies on setting yourself up the right way from the get-go to save headaches down the line.

FINAL THOUGHTS

This product is for a Mac addict. If you can live without your Mac, go with one of the other versions listed below.

QUICKBOOKS ONLINE

WHO'S IT FOR?

QuickBooks Online is designed for anyone to access. You can access the same file from a PC, Mac, or even from your smartphone (yes, you can even code your bank feed from your smartphone). Simply put, QuickBooks Online allows access from all your computer devices.

WHERE DOES IT LIVE?

The file lives in the world of Intuit (the QuickBooks parent company). It is likely on an Amazon server either in Virginia or Northern

California, depending on your location. In layman's terms, it lives in the cloud.

WHAT FEATURES ARE INCLUDED?

All of the basic QuickBooks features are included. This ranges from customers, journal entries, bank feeds, bank reconciliations, and so on. Some of the more advanced features that Pro, Premier, and Enterprise users might expect are not included.

WHAT FEATURES ARE FORGOTTEN?

All of the robust find features, advanced sorting features, and a lot of other features considered the norm for the desktop products are missing. Business owners who have used the desktop products for years often find the transition to QBO very difficult.

WHAT'S IT COST?

The online version is comparable to the desktop versions. It starts at $20 per month, which comes out to about $240 annually. If you prefer more features—such as the ability to send estimates, have multiple users, and track inventory—the price will increase.

IS IT USER-FRIENDLY?

QuickBooks Online is like all software-as-a-service products you would experience in today's world. A software-as-a-service product is an application, like one on your smart phone, where both the software and the data are provided to a customer for a recurring fee. The user interface is friendly and fairly simple. Overall, the software is simpler and easier to navigate from the start.

WHAT ELSE DO YOU NEED TO KNOW ABOUT THIS SOFTWARE?

This QuickBooks Online software is really designed for a small business owner just starting out. If you have one stream of revenue, a few bills, and a small list of expenses, this is the perfect software for you. It also allows for you to pay monthly versus a larger upfront fee.

FINAL THOUGHTS

QuickBooks Online is very solid small business accounting software. If this is your first foray into restaurant accounting, it will give you all you need. If you have multiple locations, need complex invoicing, and plan on having a few staff members in your accounting departments—the products to follow are best for you.

QUICKBOOKS PRO DESKTOP

WHO'S IT FOR?

QuickBooks Desktop Pro is the most basic of the PC versions of QuickBooks Desktop. This is accounting software focused on small businesses that use a PC.

WHERE DOES IT LIVE?

The file can live on your desktop, on a server, or in the cloud. The cloud storage has additional costs associated with it.

WHAT FEATURES ARE INCLUDED?

All the basic features you would expect from accounting software are included. You can enter customers, vendors, perform journal entries, reconciliations, and so on.

WHAT FEATURES ARE FORGOTTEN?

The main features missing in QuickBooks Pro are the ability to perform business specific reports, create and manage budgets, and to track 1099 contractors. Additionally, the inventory features are not as advanced as the higher versions of QuickBooks and could be challenging if you have a complex product that you resell (this usually does not apply to restaurant accounting). Historical reconciliations are also excluded from the Pro version; this means you better save your reports monthly and file them away.

WHAT'S IT COST?
QuickBooks Pro costs an initial fee of $299. The annual subscription runs the same price. Hosting through QuickBooks also has additional costs associated with it.

IS IT USER-FRIENDLY?
Desktop versions of QuickBooks are moderately user-friendly. Out of the box, there are a vast number of decisions the designated administrator must make, and initially this can be overwhelming. However, there are a handful of PC keyboard tricks that make it very user-friendly for PC addicts.

WHAT ELSE DO YOU NEED TO KNOW ABOUT THIS SOFTWARE?
The QuickBooks Pro software is really designed for a small restaurant owner who prefers desktop software and is just starting out. The Pro version is great for one stream of revenue, a few bills, and a small list of expenses. It is also great as you grow your staff and add complexity to your accounting.

FINAL THOUGHTS
Overall, QuickBooks Pro is solid software focused on your current and future small business needs. It's a cost-effective solution for a very small team with fewer than three users and no need for creating and emailing sales orders. Initially the software is a bit overwhelming, but this book makes it less intimidating.

· ·

PRO TIP

Once your QuickBooks Pro file is generated, you can always upgrade to Premier or Enterprise.

· ·

QUICKBOOKS PREMIER DESKTOP

WHO'S IT FOR?

QuickBooks Premier is a more advanced version of QuickBooks Desktop. This is accounting software focused on small businesses that are growing and have expanding needs. Additionally, this is for users who prefer to use PC-based software.

WHERE DOES IT LIVE?

The file can live on your desktop, on a server, or in the cloud. The cloud storage has an additional cost associated with it.

WHAT FEATURES ARE INCLUDED?

All the basic features you would expect from accounting software are included, plus much more. You can enter customers, vendors, perform journal entries, reconciliations, and so on. Additionally, QuickBooks Premier offers 50+ additional reporting options above QuickBooks Pro. You also have the ability to have up to five users work simultaneously.

WHAT FEATURES ARE FORGOTTEN?

QuickBooks Premier is very robust and covers most of the features needed to successfully account for your small business. The items that are forgotten are complex reporting and tracking features for small businesses that are scaling—these solutions can only be found in QuickBooks Enterprise.

WHAT'S IT COST?

QuickBooks Premier is $499 for a one-time software fee. The annual subscription is required and runs the same price every year after that. Hosting through QuickBooks also has additional costs associated with it.

IS IT USER-FRIENDLY?

Desktop versions of QuickBooks are moderately user-friendly. Out of the box, there are a vast number of decisions the designated administrator must make, and initially this can be overwhelming. However, there are a handful of PC keyboard tricks that make it very user-friendly for PC addicts.

WHAT ELSE DO YOU NEED TO KNOW ABOUT THIS SOFTWARE?

QuickBooks Premier is really designed for a restaurant owner who prefers desktop software and is past the basic phase of their business. Premier is great for multiple streams of revenue, many bills, and any number of expenses. It is also robust and designed for an accounting team of five.

FINAL THOUGHTS

Overall, QuickBooks Premier is solid software focused on the needs of your growing small business now and in the future. It's a cost-effective solution that is great for smaller teams of up to five users. Initially the software is a bit overwhelming, but this book makes it less so.

QUICKBOOKS ENTERPRISE

WHO'S IT FOR?
QuickBooks Enterprise is the most advanced version of QuickBooks on the market. This product's core consumer is a complex small- to midsize business with multiple individuals in the accounting department.

WHERE DOES IT LIVE?
This product could live on your corporate server or in the Intuit cloud.

WHAT FEATURES ARE INCLUDED?
All the basic QuickBooks features are included and much more. Ever think you would like to track one million customers? Need 30 staff members working in QuickBooks at once? Need consolidated financial reports? QuickBooks Enterprise does all those things and has features built in to do even more.

WHAT FEATURES ARE FORGOTTEN?
In terms of QuickBooks, no features are forgotten. However, if you are considering QuickBooks Enterprise, you need to take a deep look at your firm's needs. QuickBooks Enterprise is robust software, but it is not nearly as robust as financial enterprise resource planning (ERP) software on the market.

WHAT'S IT COST?
Depending on whether or not hosting is included and how many users need access, the product price can range from $150 to $1,000 per month. I am talking about real robust accounting needs, and the price reflects that.

IS IT USER-FRIENDLY?

The more basic features of QuickBooks Enterprise are similar to that of other QuickBooks products. They are easy to use and easy to learn. The more complex features of Enterprise can be challenging and take some time to learn for an untrained accountant.

WHAT ELSE DO YOU NEED TO KNOW ABOUT THIS SOFTWARE?

QuickBooks Enterprise is a robust software and the most advanced version of Intuit's QuickBooks product lines. This software is for expanding businesses that are outgrowing all the other basic products and need to manage lots of data or need to report on multiple entities. This is the most advanced QuickBooks software before transitioning to a truly custom accounting software such as an ERP.

- -

A QUICK ASIDE

For those of you who operate or plan to operate different entities (for example, you have an LLC for your cookbooks, an LLC for your restaurant, an S Corp for your management firm, etc.) you will need to understand the costs associated with choosing a version of QuickBooks software. The online version of QuickBooks charges you on a per-entity basis. So, if you plan to manage multiple legal entities with QuickBooks, you really should look long and hard at the versions of QuickBooks Desktop before taking the leap with QuickBooks Online.

- -

CONCLUSION

Often owners and operators get caught up in the little decisions. For example, which QuickBooks software should I use? All the above QuickBooks products are great and will help you drive your business forward. This chapter helps you choose the best version of the software by outlining the many features, nuisances, and pricing options of each version. That said, all of the software outlined in this chapter will help you accomplish your goal, the goal to account better for your restaurant.

3

COMMON ACCOUNTING
TERMS FOR RESTAURANTS

BACK TO ACCOUNTING BASICS

Not all of us had the pleasure of taking basic accounting or multiple accounting courses thereafter. The following chapter serves as a reference guide to ensure that all readers are on the same page. By covering most of the basic accounting terminology, I can ensure that you will begin approaching and understanding complex issues like an accountant. If you are already an accounting pro, feel free to skip ahead.

RELEVANCE FOR THE RESTAURANT OWNER

Even if you have all the relevant accounting prerequisites, this chapter has a neat feature in which I include a "Restaurant Industry Context" under each definition, with the simple goal of making the accounting term relevant to your day-to-day operations. So, if you're tempted to skip this chapter because you're already familiar with accounting basics, consider reading it for a refresher. If, on the other hand, you are overwhelmed by what you don't know about accounting, remember that accounting concepts are often much simpler than meets the eye: Most of accounting does not go above the mathematical level of basic algebra. Further, I've made these terms as approachable as possible so that any restaurant owner, operator, or restaurant accountant can quickly grasp them.

WHY ALL THESE FUNNY WORDS?

Oftentimes industry professionals develop their own language. While this may have initially enabled professionals to communicate better with their peers, it often turns into a barrier to entry. In accounting, the many confusing terms and analogies seem to share a goal of keeping outsiders out.

Do you need to pay a professional $500 or more an hour if you can figure out the answers to accounting questions yourself? Absolutely not. You don't need a high-level professional to understand much of what is going on in your business. You just need to better understand the terms and the associated ideas behind them.

THE LIST

ACCOUNTS PAYABLE

Accounts payable (A/P) is the amount a business owes its suppliers or creditors. Oftentimes these are debts that must be paid off within a given period to avoid default. On many companies' balance sheets, accounts payable is often logged as a current liability.

The payable is essentially a short-term IOU from the business to another business, which acts as a creditor.

 Restaurant Industry Context: Accounts payable is created when you enter a bill from your food, liquor, or beer supplier. This amount increases when you add a bill and decreases when you pay a bill.

ACCOUNTS RECEIVABLE

Accounts receivable (A/R) is the amount a business is owed by its customers. This number fluctuates over the course of the business and should be reviewed often. On your company's balance sheet, accounts receivable is often logged as an asset.

 Restaurant Industry Context: Most restaurants do not maintain an accounts receivable. However, this could occur if you hold an event, like a private dinner or a catering function, in which the customer pays you at a later date.

ACCRUAL BASIS ACCOUNTING

Accrual Basis Accounting refers to one of the two major accounting methods. Accrual basis accounting is a method that records revenues and expenses when they are incurred, regardless of when cash is received or disbursed. The term "accrual" refers to any individual entry recording revenue or expense in the absence of a cash transaction. One example of this would be invoicing a customer but not yet receiving payment—the invoice is recorded as revenue, but the cash transaction has yet to occur. Another example would be entering an invoice before payment has been remitted.

 Restaurant Industry Context: Accrual basis accounting is the simple concept of recording payroll expense with the associated sales it produced. For example, by recording last week's sales against last week's payroll expense, you can actually see if you made a profit last week. It is important to record payroll expenses and associated sales. If comparing payroll expenses to sales from different time periods, you will be unable to determine the restaurant's profitability from week to week.

ASSET

An asset describes any resource of economic value that a company owns. Yes, your truck is an asset if it is owned by the company. The money you used to build out the fixtures and furnishings in your store is also an asset. The computer equipment that sits on your desk is an asset, and so on and so forth.

 Restaurant Industry Context: Common assets for your restaurant are the ovens, hood, kitchen build out, chairs in the dinner room and so forth. Additionally, cash and money in the bank are considered assets, and are more commonly referred to as current assets. Fixed assets can be a bit trickier, so I will spend more time discussing this below.

BALANCE SHEET

A company's balance sheet gives a snapshot of the company's financial health at a given moment. This includes the cash it has on hand, its bank account balances, the liabilities it has outstanding, and the equity the owners have in the business.

 Restaurant Industry Context: The balance sheet holds lots of valuable information for a snapshot in time. For example, you can quickly see how much cash you have, how many credit card deposits are pending, how much you owe in sales tax, and how much cash you have for a certain day. Spending time on the balance sheet will always help you better manage your cash flow.

BOTTOM LINE

This is the total amount a business has made or lost at the end of a given period. The reference to "bottom" describes the relative location of the net income on a company's income statement. The term can also be used in the context of a business's earnings increasing or decreasing.

 Restaurant Industry Context: Simply put, did you make money or lose money? That is your "bottom line" and the slang phrase for the number at the bottom of the income statement or profit-and-loss statement. It is the income or loss left over after all expenses and cost of goods have been recorded.

CASH BASIS ACCOUNTING

Cash basis accounting refers to the other major accounting method. Unlike accrual basis accounting, the cash basis accounting approach recognizes revenues and expenses at the time physical cash is actually received or paid out. When transactions are recorded on a cash basis, they affect a company's books only when a completed exchange of value has occurred. Therefore, and in the short term, cash basis accounting is less accurate than accrual accounting.

 Restaurant Industry Context: Cash basis accounting is likely how you manage your books now—recording money as it comes in and as it goes out. But this approach makes it very hard to track true profitability and causes problems when making educated decisions about your business.

CASH FLOW

This is usually defined by investors as being the fundamental metric to a firm's financial health. Cash flow is really the difference between what you report on your financial statements that is not cash and cash transactions that actually occur.

In the accrual method of accounting, you are allowed to count your chickens before they hatch. This means that you can record money coming in and expenses leaving before the physical cash transaction actually occurs. For example, when you create an invoice, the sale has occurred, but really do you have the money yet? No! Cash flow reverses out all these items and gives you a true understanding of your real dollars in hand. This is oftentimes displayed in a statement of cash flows.

 Restaurant Industry Context: Cash flow refers to the money that flows through your business. Sometimes, such as during the slow season, the money you owe vendors increases. Sometimes, such as during the busy season, that money decreases. A cash flow statement helps you track where all your money is going. For example, perhaps you recently made some updates in the kitchen, purchasing a new fixed asset (like a new oven), the cash flow statement will help you realize where the funds went. The income

statement still showed similar profitability, but under accrual accounting, the new oven was classified as a fixed asset on the balance sheet. This means the cash still left your bank account, but the cash flow statement helps you understand this flow of cash and why your bank account feels drained or enlarged.

DEBT

Similar to your house mortgage, a debt is money owed on an asset. A debt in business could mean a loan, a line of credit, or money you borrowed from your mother. Better keep these debts in check to make sure your business stays healthy.

 Restaurant Industry Context: Debt is money owed to another business or person. Money spent on a credit card or taken out through a line of credit is considered debt. More complex debt can be long-term notes either from banks or other businesses.

DEPRECIATION

Large expenditures, such as the purchase of a vehicle or building, will add value to the business over an extended period. Accounting treats these purchases differently and will make them an expense over their usable life. For example, a vehicle will likely serve your business for seven years, so you will take an annual expense for this vehicle over seven years. Over time, a business' assets decrease in value due to the time that has passed since the purchase. For tax purposes, a business can recover the cost of that depreciation through a deduction. Because depreciation can be complicated, consult with your CPA to set a depreciation schedule and ensure you are depreciating all your assets correctly.

 Restaurant Industry Context: Getting a restaurant up and running is both time consuming and expensive. That $100,000 kitchen build out, it came from somewhere, likely you (perhaps

even as a personal guaranteed loan from you) or your investor's pocket. Depreciation allows you to expense (reduce your tax burden) over the course of the business for that initial outlay. It works the same conceptually for the purchase of a new oven, tables, company vehicle, and much more. The upfront cost gets amortized (spread out) over the life of the fixed asset, allowing you to annually deduct the expense from your tax liability.

EXPENSES

Business expenses are the costs the company incurs in order to operate. These are such things as rent, utilities, professional and legal fees, employee wages, contractor pay, and marketing and advertising costs.

 Restaurant Industry Context: This could be as simple as the chef running to the store to get some lemons or as complex as the weekly payroll. Expenses come in all shapes and forms: They are all in the form of owing another person or business money.

JOURNAL ENTRY

A journal entry is a transaction that occurs in the accounting records for a business. QuickBooks is designed to let you simply enter the bill, its details, including amounts and vendor information. Behind all that is the journal entry, which actually adjusts items within the general ledger. When a real business transaction occurs, such as the purchase of raw chicken, a journal entry records this transaction and then functions as the activity behind something like selecting the option to enter a bill in QuickBooks. Lucky for you, QuickBooks is designed so that most things can be done without inputting separate journal entries. These journal entry transactions are then consolidated in the general ledger and used to create financial statements.

The logic behind a journal entry is that it records the two effects of a transaction. If you purchase said chicken, you reduce your cash on hand by simultaneously recording the expense on the income statement—essentially, each transaction requires two entries. In the world of accounting, every action must have a counterbalance: For every credit there must be a debit. This is how accounting ensures everything balances and ties back to the basic accounting equation.

 Restaurant Industry Context: You will likely not use a lot of journal entries (except for where I outline them relating to sales and payroll), but they are the core function of what happens behind the scenes of your accounting software. Think about them as your restaurant manager—they help make everything related to your finances come together in a legible format.

HOUSE ACCOUNT

This is an informal name for an accounts receivable account. Accounts receivable (A/R) is the amount a business is owed by its customers. This number fluctuates over the course of the business and should be reviewed often. A good example of A/R in action is in the situation of extending credit, or allowing a customer to come in and pay later, perhaps after receiving a monthly invoice for the previous month's charges. The house account can also lend credit to certain customers, allowing them to pay at a later date. Although house accounts are very popular for businesses related to or located in hotels or resorts, I advise my clients to refrain from this practice as much as possible.

 Restaurant Industry Context: Joe, your cousin, is a regular at your restaurant. His income fluctuates and so does his interest in paying his tab. His bills are usually sent to the house account and squared up every few months, when you call Joe's mother.

House accounts are very popular in the hotel/resort arena and are valuable in making a stay a seamless experience.

LIABILITY

This is simply an obligation to repay debt. Oftentimes this is similar to a loan or line of credit. But a liability goes a bit farther and can include sales tax you owe the government or payroll taxes you owe the state.

 Restaurant Industry Context: Oftentimes, you may open a line of credit to get through the slow months—this is a liability. Money collected to be paid later—such as payroll taxes or sales tax—are liabilities as well.

NET INCOME

In the most basic sense, net income means a company's total earnings or profit. You start with income, meaning money from the sales of services or goods. You minus out COGS, the expense for creating that sales or good; then, you minus out everything else you spent money on—such as gas for the truck, a manager to run the store, etc. All that is left (which I hope for your sake is a lot) is your net income. Oh, and by the way, an increase in net income is usually a good thing!

 Restaurant Industry Context: This is the money (hopefully a profit) left over after you pay for the food, the staff who cooks the food, the staff who serves the customers, the rent, the utilities, and all other miscellaneous expenses.

POINT OF SALE, OR POS

A POS system, or point of sale, is a combination of hardware and software built to manage the business operations that are both consumer facing and back-office facing. POS manages the transactions for your business, including credit card processing, and the post-transaction operations that lead to order fulfillment.

 Restaurant Industry Context: The POS is the main hub of your business. There are many manufacturers and retailers of these products, and you may even refer to it simply as a register. The front-of-house staff enters the orders into it, the system tells the back-of-house what food to make, and then the customer is checked out on the same equipment.

PROFIT AND LOSS (INCOME STATEMENT)

Also known as a profit and loss statement, an income statement shows the profitability of a business during a period of time. The income statement looks at a business's revenues, cost of goods, and expenses through all of its activities (including all bank accounts, credit cards, etc.).

 Restaurant Industry Context: The profit and loss statement will tell you how your business did in the month of July. It will tell you if you made or lost money during a specific period by taking into account sales, cost of goods, and expenses.

RETAINED EARNINGS

This is the amount of net earnings not paid out as owner/partner distributions but retained by the company (precisely why it is called "retained" earnings). It can be found under shareholders' equity on the balance sheet. This will be clearly outlined in the coming chapter, as it is an integral part of your chart of accounts.

 Restaurant Industry Context: This is the money left in the business after you calculate net income and distribute money to owners/partners.

CONCLUSION

Why did I just bore you with all these terms? Simply because to grow your knowledge base, we must have the basic vocabulary framework. This chapter outlined all the terminology that you will come across in the coming pages. Additionally, understanding important accounting terms in a restaurant related context will only serve to better allow for you to interface with both this book and the accounting professionals you will come across throughout your restaurant's operation. Now that the baseline has been established, we can expound on it and start getting your restaurant set up for accounting success.

4

CHART OF ACCOUNTS FOR RESTAURANTS

LEARN TO LOVE THE CHART OF ACCOUNTS

One of the core hearts of any accounting software, QuickBooks included, is to track the transactions that occur within your business. These transactions are tracked based on which chart of accounts category they are classified to, essentially making the chart of accounts the most important part of any accounting software, particularly QuickBooks—because without a heart you cannot survive.

With all the other tasks in a restaurant that need to be managed (for example, the hundred-plus guests coming to dinner tonight), setting up a great chart of accounts can seem completely nominal. However, learning to create and nurture a great chart of accounts will serve to expedite any accounting-related task while simultaneously increasing the quality of your financial reporting. Yes, the chart of accounts is that important, so I recommend paying attention to this chapter.

A RESTAURANT CHART OF ACCOUNTS

In business school, apprenticeships, and self-trainings, most of the literature and many of the illustrative examples treat businesses generally. Ever notice that there are only a few books on QuickBooks restaurant accounting but many on general QuickBooks small business? That's because most business owners fail to value industry-specific knowledge the way they should. Industry-specific knowledge allows you to get ahead of the bell curve, run your business more efficiently, and, most importantly, spend less time on menial tasks. The goal of the chart of accounts, similar to the goal of this book, is to streamline the restaurant accounting process using QuickBooks, so do just that by creating a great chart of accounts specific to your restaurant business. Do it by understanding and utilizing the coming chapter.

MISE EN PLACE

Because you work in the restaurant industry, you intimately understand the French culinary phrase *mise en place*, meaning "putting in place" or "everything in its place." A proper chart of accounts functions the same way as an organized restaurant station. Everything has its proper place, and everything is conveniently located. Simply put, a chart of accounts will add value to your business if it is set up properly.

Most accounting software comes preloaded with a few different chart of accounts templates. When you open QuickBooks, for example, you will be asked what industry you operate within, and then you will be given a preset chart of accounts. The offerings may have too many accounts and subaccounts, or it may have too few. Ninety-five percent of the time this chart of accounts is not designed for a growing restaurant like yours, so look below to find a solid, applicable example.

The plate is often considered the canvas for creating a fine meal— without the well-crafted ingredients of every dish, it would be simply a plate. While the chart of accounts functions as a mise en place, it is also the canvas for your financial back-office operations. It offers a framework for you to build upon, but without the proper ingredients and attention, it, too, will fail you. From the colors to the texture, to finishing touches and cleanliness, what makes an amazing dish is a killer presentation that functions as the culmination of all the ingredients and effort that went into it. In an organized finance department, the chart of accounts is the plate on which ingredients and effort (like proper sales and expense recording, payroll setup, and more) come together.

THE IMPORTANCE OF THE CHART OF ACCOUNTS

I hear people harp on the importance of some preferred method or another: You must do *this*, or you must do *that*, or you have to do this *other thing* in order to be successful. While the majority of entrepreneurs have probably heard this advice and then followed their own path, the chart of accounts is actually crucial to the success of every business—including restaurants—so, what you've heard is true, you really must do it.

A good chart of accounts makes your life easier in both a business analysis and a tax reporting context. Let's say you run a complex restaurant business and have waitstaff on the floor, management for waitstaff, employees in the kitchen, and kitchen managers, too. Although all of the above items are payroll expenses for your small restaurant, business decisions cannot be made by looking at that number in total. Business decisions must instead be made by tracking each department's payroll expenses for both management and hourly as a percentage of total sales, so you can see the fluctuations both in aggregate total numbers and as a percentage of sales. The chart of accounts helps you see these numbers. By breaking up payroll expenses into departments and even roles (such as management versus nonmanagement), you will be able to see on a weekly, monthly, quarterly, and yearly basis how productive your team is, how much revenue was created by payroll expenses, and how much product was added to inventory by payroll expenses.

Let's take this example a step further. By focusing on the week-over-week expense for these departments and roles, you should be able to establish a minimum operating expense and, respectively, a quality operating percentage for when the business gets busy. By correctly configuring your chart of accounts and running regular daily and weekly reporting, you can start to pinpoint business drivers and business losers. More waitstaff is obviously necessary as business picks up, but it is more valuable to make some customers wait five minutes than lose money on a given day. By extrapolating related numbers with an in-depth chart of accounts from which you can run actual reports, you will be able to make better business decisions.

Ultimately, a well-established chart of accounts in QuickBooks helps you run your business better. How much are you spending on kitchen supplies? How much is your payroll costing you? How many refunds did you have last week? How many comps are the front of the house issuing? All these answers can be pulled from a quality chart of accounts, so pay attention!

THE CHART OF ACCOUNTS STRUCTURE

The chart of accounts is designed to help you organize your business income and expenses. The chart of accounts is unique to every business and can include only a handful of accounts or can include thousands. The quantity of accounts depends solely on how the business prefers to set up the accounts. Keep in mind, by keeping your chart of accounts lean, you can easily and quickly read key reports like your profit and loss statement. The profit and loss statement is a subsection of the main chart of accounts and is created by QuickBooks using certain accounts in your chart of accounts. The profit and loss statement shows the profitability of a business during a certain period of time, and—unlike a payroll expenses report—it's more useful when it includes only broad categories. Ultimately, a lean chart of accounts can be used to generate both more complicated reports and more simple reports. If you're looking for more detailed information on certain accounts, then look to the reporting features in QuickBooks, not the chart of accounts.

PRO TIP

At the end of the year, if any of your income or expense categories shows a very small amount, consider combining that category into another category to keep your chart of accounts as short as possible.

STANDARDIZE THE CHART OF ACCOUNTS *(and Make Your CPA Happy)*

I hear it all the time: How do I standardize my chart of accounts or make the chart of accounts comply with Generally Accepted Accounting Principles? Below I highlight some of the common procedures for standardization, but remember that one of the major goals of accounting is to serve the business owner's needs—so make your chart of accounts work for you.

A standard chart of accounts is organized according to a numerical system. Remember when you learned to count to 10 as a child? I am going to help you relearn how to do that, but this time each number is going to mean something different.

Each major category begins with a certain number, and then each subcategory within that major category begins with the same number. For example, if assets are classified by numbers starting with the digit 1, then cash accounts might be labeled 1001, accounts receivable might be labeled 1002, inventory might be labeled 1003, and so on. If liabilities accounts are classified by numbers starting with the digit 2, then accounts payable might be labeled 2001, short-term debt might be labeled 2002, and so on.

Depending on the size and complexity of your restaurant, the chart of accounts may include a few dozen accounts, or it may include a hundred.

Below is a quick cheat sheet to help you structure your chart of accounts.

• •

1000 – 1999 Assets

2000 – 2999 Liabilities

3000 – 3999 Equity

4000 – 4999 Income or Revenue

5000 – 5999 Cost of Goods Sold

6000 – 7999 Expenses

8000 – 8999 Other Income

9000 – 9999 Other Expenses

• •

CHART OF ACCOUNTS CATEGORIES

At this point you may be in information overload mode and completely overwhelmed. Don't fret—it is not as complicated as you think, especially in QuickBooks. You may have heard some of the structural categories above or not. In the coming paragraphs I will dive into each one in a simple format to help you better understand them.

ASSETS: 1000 – 1999

Assets are items that your company owns. For example, you could own the money in your bank account or own the computer you are reading this book on. Assets are usually divided into two categories—current assets and fixed assets—and QuickBooks helps you with this division.

Current assets are items that can quickly be turned into cash, such as the money in your bank account. (Of course, even though you can put your car on Craigslist and quickly sell the clunker, it is not considered a current asset.) Some other items that may be current assets are savings accounts, money market accounts, accounts receivable, and inventory. Yes, that's right, your food and beverage inventory is a current asset.

Fixed assets are items you would usually have to sell to generate cash. The minimum amount for fixed assets is often $500. Some examples of these items are that clunker mentioned above, machinery, equipment, computer, cars, and so on. When building out a restaurant, the kitchen and related appliances are often classified as fixed assets.

LIABILITIES: 2000 – 2999

Liabilities are the money your company owes other people. Did you borrow $1,000 from your buddy to cover payroll on that week sales were slow? Well, that would be a liability for your entity. Do you collect sales tax that you need to remit to the government? That's a liability because you owe that money—it's not yours. Tip money collected for employees to be redistributed back to them on their checks is considered a liability, as well. Do you make major purchases with your company credit card, those are liabilities, too.

EQUITY: 3000 – 3999

Equity accounts really depend on how your entity is structured, and they vary depending on if your entity is a sole proprietorship (single member LLC), partnership (multiple member LLC), or corporation.

In QuickBooks, if your entity is a sole proprietorship, you need a capital account and an owner's draw account, which are both equity accounts and are therefore categorized under the equity portion of the balance sheet and chart of accounts. The capital account is to keep track of just that, the total capital (or amount of money) you have invested since starting the business, plus or minus the net profit or loss each year since you started the business. Use the owner's draw account for money you take out of the business for personal use, such as paying your car note or for an Xbox for little Jimmy, for cash withdrawals, your distributions, and any money that gets deposited into your personal accounts.

- -

PRO TIP

Note that as a sole proprietor (single member LLC) you do not pay yourself as a regular employee via W-2. You need to distribute that money and pay taxes on the businesses net income. Consult with your CPA to ensure you are following the correct protocol.

- -

If your company is a partnership (think multimember LLC) or Limited Liability Partnership (LLP), you need to set up capital and draw accounts for each partner in QuickBooks under the equity category in the chart of accounts. For example, did Uncle Todd give you some money to start your business, and did your wife's dad Joe also kick in some cash? They would need QuickBooks accounts titled

Uncle Todd's Capital and Uncle Todd's Draw. Similarly, Joe would need Wife's Dad Joe Capital and Wife's Dad Joe Draw. As an aside, the money contributed to open the business goes into the capital account and the money distributed goes into the draw account.

If your company is an S or C corporation or an LLC corporation (different from an LLC partnership), the chart of accounts should have a common stock account and sometimes a preferred stock account. Common stock and preferred stock represent the total sum of stock the company has issued. An LLC might have member stock if there is more than one person who owns stock. This is on a bit more complex level, however, so you should refer to your CPA to ensure you set up these accounts correctly based on your entity type and member structure.

INCOME OR REVENUE: 4000 – 4999

Income or revenue is the income your business gets from day-to-day business operations. These include but are not limited to: food sales, beverage sales, catering sales, and service fees you collect. Structuring these accounts in the chart of accounts in QuickBooks is really up to you. Perhaps you run two different departments for your business, such as the front-of-the-house and the back-of-the-house, in this case, you may want to separate them into subaccounts of income as is done for the food and beverage department outlined below. Or maybe you have multiple revenue centers such as a large to-go business and a full-service sit-down restaurant; in this case, separating the two will help you better manage your operation. If you want to see the performance for each department's subcategories, then you may want to use sub-subaccounts. Either way, it's best to remember that less is more. Remember, the goal is to fit your income statement on one page, which means fewer accounts from the chart of accounts.

Then, you will be able to track the health and performance of your business in a simple one-take.

Oftentimes, refunds and exchanges also live in the Income and revenue category. This ensures that your next profit is truly your next profit. Your top line revenue number should be the money you received for the period, not the money received before refunds and item comps.

COST OF GOODS SOLD (AKA COGS): 5000 – 5999

In QuickBooks, the cost of goods sold includes the cost of raw materials, freight charges for getting raw material to a warehouse, labor for building the finished goods, and freight charges for getting the goods to the customer. For a restaurant business, the main inputs are the food and beverages inputs purchased to produce the dishes and drinks on the menu. Some operators prefer to see one lump sum of purchases, while others choose to break out purchases into their main inputs of meat, dairy, baked goods, and dry goods. I recommend the latter as it lets you better manage the purchasing process. When setting up the COGS category in the chart of accounts, be creative: Feel free to add additional expense accounts, consolidate accounts, create subaccounts and more. Basically, figure out what will make your business function better, set guidelines, and follow them.

EXPENSES: 6000 – 7999

Expenses are the fixed costs that exist even if you sell no products or services. Examples include rent, telephone, insurance, vehicle expense, advertising, and utilities.

OTHER INCOME: 8000 – 8999

Other income in QuickBooks is income you earn outside the

normal way you do business, including interest income, gain on the sale of an asset, insurance settlement, a stock sale, or rents from buildings you own when real estate is not your main business focus.

As a restaurant owner, it is likely that you will not use this income type very often.

OTHER EXPENSES: 9000 – 9999

The other expenses category refers to an expense that is outside of your normal business, such as a loss on the sale of an asset, or stockbroker fees (though it is not limited to these items and also often includes depreciation, amortization, R&D expenses, finance cost, and income tax expense). Not sure how to classify something? Check with your CPA—a great CPA knows that the more questions they answer throughout the year, the easier tax time will be on them.

THE GENERAL LEDGER

For all general purposes, the chart of accounts in QuickBooks is very similar to a general ledger. To be more precise, the general ledger is the numbered accounts based off the chart of accounts, and it stores all the financial transactions for the life of your firm. A general ledger account is an account or record used to sort and store balance sheet and income statement transactions. This is where all the transactions entered inside QuickBooks live. From invoices to payments to sales, the general ledger keeps a record of all these transactions. The general ledger lives inside QuickBooks, but is also a common accounting-based report across all accounting software. A restaurant owner or manager should review the general ledger monthly to ensure that all transactions are properly representative of their business and are classified correctly. Examples of general ledger accounts include everything from cash and bank accounts to salary expense and revenue.

Let's say you wanted to see what has gone on in your restaurant over the past six months. Well, obviously you sit in the restaurant or kitchen and see what is going on in your business. More importantly, you want to see what your company is spending your hard-earned money on, so you use QuickBooks to run the general ledger report.

In QuickBooks, the general ledger report shows all the transactions that have taken place within your business and the codes under which these items were classified. The report really paints a picture of what is going on in your firm, answering questions such as, *why are my advertising expenses so high for the year*? and, *what is going on with my payroll*? Running the general ledger report for a longer period lets you see the fluctuations of certain expenses over that period. For example, has your weekly payroll run doubled? Did the new staff result in a hit in profitability? Did your daily sales revenue decline during the summer?

Taking a look at the general ledger report lets you get very granular about your business and what is going on within it. Reviewing this report also ensures that your staff or you have been recording transactions properly. The general ledger report shows all your top reports—think income statement and balance sheet details in a detailed overview. This can be overwhelming at first, but once you get used to the format you can see all your accounting related transactions in one place! Are all your credit card fees in the right place? Or, do you accidentally have all your payroll expenses in the legal and professional fees category and legal and professional fees in the payroll expense category?

. . . .

PRO TIP

Setting up a proper chart of accounts is the first step in making sure your general ledger is in order! Once that's set up, you just need to quickly review this report on a monthly or quarterly basis. This makes the closing of the year and preparing of your tax returns a breeze come March. Remember, plan for success, or don't plan and fail.

. . . .

SAMPLE CHART OF ACCOUNTS

Below you will find a detailed chart of accounts. This is a sample specifically for restaurant businesses. Though not always inclusive, this should be informative enough to set you on your way to restaurant accounting success.

1000	Cash On Hand	Bank
1010	Bank Account 1	Bank
1020	Bank Account 2	Bank
1030	Bank Account 3	Bank
1100	Accounts Receivable (A/R)	Accounts receivable (A/R)
1150	Credit Card Receivable	Other Current Assets
1175	House Account	Other Current Assets
1200	Inventory	Other Current Assets

1210	Inventory: Food Inventory	Other Current Assets
1220	Inventory: Beverage Inventory	Other Current Assets
1230	Inventory: Bar & Consumable Inventory	Other Current Assets
1400	Prepaid Expenses	Other Current Assets
1500	Fixed Asset Computers	Fixed Assets
1530	Furniture & Fixtures	Fixed Assets
1540	Leasehold Improvements	Fixed Assets
1600	Accumulated Depreciation	Fixed Assets
1700	Capitalized Start Up Expenses	Fixed Assets
1800	Security Deposits	Other Assets
2000	Accounts Payable (A/P)	Accounts payable (A/P)
2110	Credit Card 1	Credit Card
2120	Credit Card 2	Credit Card
2130	Credit Card 3	Credit Card
2210	Sales Tax Expense	Other Current Liabilities
2220	Payroll Clearing	Other Current Liabilities
2230	Accrued Expenses	Other Current Liabilities
2250	Payroll Liabilities	Other Current Liabilities
2280	Tips Payable	Other Current Liabilities
2300	Gift Cards Outstanding	Other Current Liabilities

2400	Notes Payable	Other Current Liabilities
3000	Capital Contribution	Equity
3010	Capital Contribution: Member A	Equity
3020	Capital Contribution: Member B	Equity
3030	Capital Contribution: Member C	Equity
3040	Capital Contribution: Member D	Equity
3300	Retained Earnings	Equity
4100	Food Sales	Income
4110	Food Sales: Lunch Sales	Income
4120	Food Sales: Dinner Sales	Income
4130	Food Sales: Food Comps	Income
4140	Food Sales: Food Discounts	Income
4200	Beverage Sales	Income
4210	Beverage Sales: N/A Beverage	Income
4220	Beverage Sales: Liquor Sales	Income
4230	Beverage Sales: Beer Sales	Income
4250	Beverage Sales: Wine Sales	Income
4260	Beverage Sales :Beverage Comps	Income
4270	Beverage Sales: Beverage Discounts	Income
4300	Service/Fee Income	Income

4400	Merchandise Sales	Income
4500	Catering & Contracts	Income
5100	Food Cost	Cost of Goods Sold
5110	Food Cost: Meat Cost	Cost of Goods Sold
5120	Food Cost: Poultry Cost	Cost of Goods Sold
5130	Food Cost: Seafood Cost	Cost of Goods Sold
5140	Food Cost: Dairy Cost	Cost of Goods Sold
5150	Food Cost: Produce Cost	Cost of Goods Sold
5160	Food Cost: Frozen Cost	Cost of Goods Sold
5170	Food Cost: Grocery Cost	Cost of Goods Sold
5190	Change in Food Inventory	Cost of Goods Sold
5200	Beverage Cost	Cost of Goods Sold
5210	Beverage Cost: N/A Beverage Cost	Cost of Goods Sold
5220	Beverage Cost: Liquor Cost	Cost of Goods Sold
5230	Beverage Cost: Beer Cost	Cost of Goods Sold
5240	Beverage Cost: Wine Cost	Cost of Goods Sold
5290	Change in Beverage Inventory	Cost of Goods Sold
5300	Merchandise Cost	Cost of Goods Sold
6000	Payroll Expenses	Expenses
6010	Payroll Expenses: FOH Wages	Expenses

6011	Payroll Expenses: FOH Wages: FOH Management	Expenses
6012	Payroll Expenses: FOH Wages: FOH Hourly	Expenses
6020	Payroll Expenses: BOH Wages	Expenses
6021	Payroll Expenses: BOH Wages: BOH Management	Expenses
6022	Payroll Expenses: BOH Wages: BOH Hourly	Expenses
6030	Payroll Expenses: Administrative Wages	Expenses
6040	Payroll Expenses: Employee Benefits	Expenses
6050	Payroll Expenses: Employee Meals	Expenses
6060	Payroll Expenses: Workman's Comp	Expenses
6065	Payroll Taxes	Expenses
6070	Payroll Expenses: Employers Payroll Taxes	Expenses
6075	Payroll Expenses: Payroll Processing Fee	Expenses
6080	Payroll Expenses: Contract Labor	Expenses
6100	Direct Operating Expenses	Expenses
6110	Direct Operating Expenses: China - Glassware - Flatware	Expenses
6120	Direct Operating Expenses: Restaurant & Kitchen Supply	Expenses
6130	Direct Operating Expenses: Cleaning Supply	Expenses
6140	Direct Operating Expenses: Decoration & Guest Supply	Expenses
6150	Direct Operating Expenses: Linen Services	Expenses
6160	Direct Operating Expenses: Permit & License	Expenses

6200	Cleaning Services	Expenses
6300	Marketing Expenses	Expenses
6400	Advertising and Promotion	Expenses
6500	Travel	Expenses
6600	Automobile Expenses	Expenses
6700	Meals & Entertainment	Expenses
6800	POS Fee	Expenses
6900	Telephone and Internet	Expenses
7000	General and Administrative	Expenses
7010	General and Administrative: Bad Debts - Over/Short	Expenses
7020	General and Administrative: Bank Fees	Expenses
7021	General and Administrative: Bank Fees: Bank Fees - Sub	Expenses
7022	General and Administrative: Bank Fees: Merchant Account Fees	Expenses
7030	General and Administrative: Insurance Expense	Expenses
7100	Legal & Professional Services	Expenses
7110	Legal & Professional Services: Accounting & Bookkeeping	Expenses
7120	Legal & Professional Services: Consulting Fees	Expenses
7130	Legal & Professional Services: Legal Fees	Expenses
7200	General and Administrative: Office Expenses	Expenses
7210	General and Administrative: Office Expenses: Dues & Subscriptions	Expenses

7220	General and Administrative: Office Expenses: Office Supplies	Expenses
7300	Facilities	Expenses
7310	Facilities: Rent & Lease	Expenses
7320	Facilities: Utilities	Expenses
7330	Facilities: Garbage Removal	Expenses
7340	Facilities: Pest Control	Expenses
7350	Facilities: Repairs and Maintenance	Expenses
7400	Equipment Rental	Expenses
7500	Sales Tax Expense	Expenses
7999	Ask My Accountant	Expenses
8100	Interest Earned	Other Income
8200	Other Miscellaneous Income	Other Income
9000	Taxes and Fees	Other Expense

The outline above is a great sample chart of accounts, and one I have used it for multiple clients. However, I modify the account to fit each client's specific situation. For instance, maybe you specialize in Eastern cuisine and offer sake instead of wine? Well, it's important that you track that, so you'd replace the wine in 5340 with sake. The same concept can be extrapolated through the rest of the chart of accounts. For example, perhaps you have five bank accounts instead of one: Use the above framework and expand!

COST OF GOODS CONFIGURATION

The cost of goods sold category (COGS) always presents a lovely debate between owners, bookkeepers, and accountants. Everyone seems to have their own opinion on this matter. For example, is payroll a COGS? I prefer to expense this as I believe looking at the components of the food and beverage program as a percentage of sales is the simplest way to ensure a quick analysis of the income statement. Additionally, particular components of invoices are heatedly debated, so make sure you have a system in place to ensure classification is consistent. In reality, you have to make COGS and your income statement work for you and your business. The above chart of accounts records all food and beverage purchases as part of COGS. I find this is the quickest and easiest way to track restaurant performance as food and beverage purchases are the main driver of your finished good.

UNDERSTAND THE VALUE OF COMPS

Comps are defined as giving something away for free. Any restaurant of any size makes mistakes, whether those mistakes happen in the front of house or the back of house. Either way, all mistakes need to be tracked. This is where the comps category can help. By recording mistakes, you can begin to understand where waste occurs and where to focus energies to resolve the issues contributing to the waste. Tracking comps—for example, tracking tickets that have been discounted to ensure a happy guest experience, even after a mistake was made—is valuable in the hospitality business.

Even further, understanding the rate of these comps and the actual dollar value associated with them and also where your restaurant should be performing compared to industry standards is truly priceless.

In the chart of accounts above, comps reduce net income and allow you to track important metrics such as food and labor cost based on the net income, also known as income after comps. This metric ensures that you are reaching your benchmarks even with comps. Comparing both gross sales operating margins and net sales margins will ensure that you see both the true cost of comps and can make executive management decisions to ensure the restaurant continues to perform better.

HOW TO TREAT COMPS

In the world of social influencers, intense marketing campaigns, and social reviews, comps are becoming more and more common. With so many different types of comps, sometimes it is hard to track the actual kitchen performance.

My recommendation is to create subaccounts to track these multiple types of comps, be it true comps, influencer marketing, or special marketing campaigns. By creating a subaccount, you can quickly modify the performance metrics for food and beverage cost and get your true operating margins.

When you treat comps as subaccounts, they become contra revenue accounts (meaning, income accounts that reduce revenue). By doing this, you ensure that your other reporting is accurate because you are no longer expensing comps, which could have ramifications on your sales tax or rent if you pay as a percentage of sales. Most importantly, for the month closing process, the top and net sales numbers reconcile to your POS system. Additionally, you can remove these items to quickly get your true cost of goods for food and beverage.

THE WORLD OF DISCOUNTS

Discounts are a reduction from the gross amount or value of something. For any growing and budding restaurant, I would hope that you already have a strong advertising and marketing program in place. This can be as simple as a local publication referring you, direct mailer coupons, return coupons, or the like.

This is also an important metric to track as it can result in abuse within the business. Coupon codes, physical coupons, and the like are easily photocopied or duplicated, allowing them to be used on cash tickets. If someone in the front of the house uses these to their advantage, they may get an extra bonus every time they use such a coupon on a cash ticket.

To better prevent this from happening and to avoid any abuse, you can watch the comp metric as a percentage of both food and beverage revenue. This will ensure that comps stay in line and aren't abused.

Additionally, tracking comps will help you see if your marketing efforts are merely driving top line sales or net revenue—the money you actually received after accounting for comps and discounts.

KEEP THINGS CONCISE

Every time I review books from within the restaurant industry, I see that almost every line item is cluttered with at least five subaccounts. For example, repair and maintenance has an elevator repair subcategory, freezer subcategory, bar subcategory, office subcategory, sidewalk subcategory, and so on.

Look, it is great to try to stay informed about your business, but if you are focusing on such granular details as which days you bought milk from what vendor, are you potentially losing sight of the big picture? The chart of accounts should offer an easy-to-access answer to one question: *How is your business doing?* Therefore, try to avoid adding unnecessary subcategories in your QuickBooks chart of accounts. Try instead to create a chart of accounts that allows you to see your entire income statement on one or two pages and therefore enables you to grasp the big picture quickly.

Yes, details are important, and QuickBooks easily lets you add both notes to transactions (think memos or expense notes) as well as run very granular reports. Are you curious about what is happening in your repair and maintenance expense category? Don't clutter up the chart of accounts. Simply dial in on that and print a QuickBooks report.

CONCLUSION

The chart of accounts is the heart of any restaurant accounting office. It will set up the business owner and operators on the path for success from day one. Knowing what to track and how to track it are as important as actually reviewing those metrics. The chart of accounts provided has a simple goal, to help you understand the performance of your prime costs (the food and labor costs). This chart of accounts sets you up to simply track those items and their related revenue centers, resulting in the ability to see the business-es performance at a glance and the related fluctuations that need to be addressed. Now that we have conquered our chart of accounts, let's move onto how to properly record sales.

5

CONQUERING DAILY SALES AND INVOICING

THE IMPORTANCE OF SALES

Understanding and recording sales properly is important for any successful enterprise. Why are sales so important? Without sales, the money to cover your prime cost, controllable expenses, and essentially any money outflow is not available. Track sales to see how your business performs month over month, year over year, day over day. In aggregate, sales are one of the vital performance metrics for your restaurant, so getting sales right is one of the most important facets of your accounting operation.

Restaurants already face multiple uphill battles to start. Recording sales should not be one of them. However, with so many different approaches available in the marketplace, it is often challenging to determine the right system to implement. This chapter has the specific goal of ensuring that sales are properly tracked, cash is properly tracked, and all this is done under the accrual method of accounting to ensure you are looking at your business's performance correctly. Because restaurants are particularly challenging, this process can be both time consuming and complex, though not necessarily for the correct reasons. This chapter will serve as a simple guide to expedite the process of daily sales, making it so simple your teenage son or daughter could handle it.

THE BACK OFFICE IS EVERYTHING

Like any business, the overall success and health is driven and maintained by what happens in the back office. I know from personal experience that a restaurant can have amazing food, a friendly staff, and an awesome location, but if the owners or operators don't have good numbers, or if they have good numbers and misunderstand them, the restaurant's run will be short-lived.

At first, tracking everything going on within multiple registers can seem complex. Add in the gift certificates, tips payable, item coding, and so on and so forth, and in a matter of minutes, proper accounting can seem overwhelming. Well, I'm here to tell you that it all is actually really simple—as long as you set up the basics correctly from day one (or modify—and understand why you're modifying—what you already have with the information below).

CHANGE YOUR CURRENT METHOD

For those who have never used QuickBooks before, sales receipts are a popular way of recording when money has been received. Unfortunately, sales receipts only record a sale in one type of payment denomination. Journal entries on the other hand record all payment types and transactions—it's basically a sales receipt on steroids.

Your restaurant could currently be entering sales a million different ways. For example, clearing net deposits, creating sales receipts, creating invoices, creating multiple journal entries, and much more. Most of these methods fail to record sales in the correct period, or fail to capture the multiple ways money is received. Additionally, they are often not configured to display sales by the different profit centers.

The method I introduce below works for a multitude of reasons. Sales are recorded under the accrual accounting method. Deposits are tracked as a receivable, ensuring that all money that is supposed to be received is actually received. Additionally, sales are classified by revenue type. All these items can be handled efficiently and accurately with one simple entry instead of multiple.

THE DAILY SALES METHOD

Daily sales are simply that, the sales that occur daily in your restaurant. If you have a point-of-sale (POS) setup, you know that you must close each shift and then each day to both ensure you have received all cash and to tell your credit card processors that the day is done and that it's time to send you your money.

Since accounting for sales in a restaurant means tracking what occurs in the POS it is important that you record sales daily. Why, you ask? Because your POS tips, credit cards, and cash are all on a daily cycle. The easiest way to account for this is to use QuickBooks to follow a similar cycle. If you run a catering business, you will need to invoice clients outside the POS system, which I will cover briefly at the end of this chapter.

In the coming chapter, I will show you how to convert all the great data your POS tracks and convert it into the language of accounting. It may be a bit confusing at first, but by capturing your daily sales properly in QuickBooks, you can ensure that everything from comps to discounts are tracked and that all necessary cash and credit card payments are received.

ACCOUNTING FOR THE DAILY SALES METHOD

Restaurant daily sales are actually fairly complex, with lots of things going on. For example, you sell both beverages and food products, and you receive payments in cash, credit cards, and gift cards. Additionally, you may receive and pay out tips now or in the future. Some of those tips are in cash and some in credit cards.

All these complex transactions can be confusing, but that is why I recommend using journal entries. This will allow you to capture all these complex events in one transaction.

What you will need to understand is how to make a simple journal entry, and debit and credit the correct accounts. There is no need to understand all the intricacies; you simply need to understand that certain balances get larger with specific actions and are similarly reduced by counter actions.

Here, I will try to make daily sales as simple as possible, I promise!

So, what exactly are journal entries? In general terms, journal entries are the root of double entry accounting. They contain the information about what happens behind your transactions in QuickBooks. When you enter an expense in QuickBooks, pay a bill, make a deposit, and so forth, you are entering numerous journal entries without actually entering them.

In practical terms, a journal entry is an accounting entry in which an account from your chart of accounts is debited and similarly an account from your chart of accounts is credited. It can contain multiple debits and multiple credits, or simply one of each. However, in either case, the debit and credit totals must equal each other. You've likely been doing journal entries all along and not even realizing it.

To give you the confidence that you can easily keep up with your journal entries, I want to walk you through recording daily sales in this manner, but in a low-stakes environment where you'll be able to catch your mistakes and effectively avoid worrying too much about debits and credits.

UTILIZE THE POS TO ENTER DAILY SALES

In most POS systems, every day, or every shift, ends with what is typically called a z-report (different POS systems might call it the day-close report, the shift report, or something else). Properly closing out at the end of the day with a z-report ensures that sales from Tuesday's big event don't accidentally show up on Friday's sales report. Essentially, this report ensures that the cash in the drawer at the end of the day matches the cash in the drawer from the beginning of the day, or, for server-specific restaurants, that the waitstaff started with $0 and ended with $0. At the end of the day, depending on how your operation is run, your report will show that your staff will either owe you money, or, if they cash out tips daily, you will owe them money.

The z-report should show all sales, including types, sales tax payable, credit card sales versus cash sales, and so on. Sometimes this information is found by combining two separate reports from your POS, this just depends on what POS is being used. Once you have the daily sales summary closed out and at your disposal, you can enter the daily sales within QuickBooks as outlined later on in this chapter.

RESTAURANT SALES JOURNAL ENTRY BASICS

Below I will walk through each account in the chart of accounts and how it will be treated in our journal entry when it is entered into QuickBooks.

Lunch Sales, Dinner Sales, N/A Beverage Sales, Liquor Sales, Beer Sales, and Wine Sales

In a QuickBooks restaurant sales journal entry, these items are treated as credits. You increase the sales on the income statement with these transactions. For example, if you sold $500 in lunch sales yesterday, when you enter it into the chart of accounts, you are crediting the journal entry $500.

FOOD COMPS AND BEVERAGE COMPS

These items are treated as debits and will therefore decrease total sales. Say you have a dinner entrée item priced at $19.99 and your customer was unhappy with the side, so you comped their dinner 50 percent, or $9.99. This transaction will reduce the dollars received, and net sales will end up being $10 instead of the sale price of $19.99. Your journal entry helps to track this.

SALES TAX PAYABLE

We all love the government and paying taxes don't we? Regardless of my sarcasm, sales tax is not a game. You have collected it, and it is due, my friend. You will therefore be crediting this account. You have received the money on behalf of the government, to be paid to them at a later date. This is money owed, which is classified as a liability on the balance sheet. By crediting this within the journal entry, the sales tax payable account on the balance sheet will increase.

GIFT CARDS

This is a tricky one! This could be entered as either a debit or a credit. It is a credit if you have sold a gift card and have redeemed none. For example, if you sell a $100 gift card, you have increased your gift card liability by $100. On the other hand, if a gift card was redeemed, you reduced this liability—meaning, if a $75 gift card was used by a customer to pay for the dinner, this will be entered as a debit and reduces your gift card liability by the same amount.

It can be a bit confusing for sure. Just remember that when you sell a gift card, you owe someone that money. When a gift card is used, you no longer owe that money. A credit increases that liability account and a debit reduces it.

TIPS PAYABLE

As you know, tips are the lifeblood of the hospitality business. They help team members pay their bills, and they let team members know if they did (or did not do) a good job. They are currently a key part of the restaurant world, and accounting for them is important.

Tips are similar to gift cards as they act as a liability on the balance sheet. When you receive tips that you owe the staff, you increase this liability, which is likely to be paid out on your employees' next paycheck. Unlike gift cards, however, tips are always a credit in the sales journal entry.

CASH ON HAND

When you sell food and receive cash, you increase your cash on hand. It is in a bank bag, on the way to the bank, or maybe sitting in the safe. Wherever it may be, cash on hand is a current asset that has been increased at the end of the day.

This current asset will be recorded as a debit and will therefore increase the amount of the asset on the balance sheet. Cash on hand poses a huge challenge for many restaurant owners, and I will explain why later in the book. In this chapter, it is enough to think of cash on hand as a debit that can help us track money received for sales.

CREDIT CARD RECEIVABLE

You sell food, and the customer pays with a credit card—now the credit card processor owes you money. This is a current asset that you hope to collect. For this account, you will debit, just as you do for cash on hand. Doing so increases this account on the balance sheet.

SALES JOURNAL EXAMPLE

ACCOUNT	DEBIT	CREDIT
4110 - Lunch Sales		$200
4120 - Dinner Sales		$200
4130 - Food Comps	$50	
4140 - Food Discounts	$50	
4310 - N/A Beverages		$100
4320 - Liquor Sales		$100
4330 - Beer Sales		$100
4350 - Wine Sales		$100
4360 - Beverage Comps	$50	
4370 - Beverage Discounts	$50	
2210 - Sales Tax Payable		$100
2300 - Gift Cards	$100	
2280 - Tips Payable		$200
1000 - Cash On Hand	$100	
1150 - Credit Card Receivable	$700	
Total	$1100	$1100

A QUICKER OVERVIEW

At first, the sales journal may seem overwhelming, but don't fret, it is actually very simple. The 4000s are all your income accounts: They record revenue or sales. The debits located in the 4000s are your comps or discounts: They reduce revenue and are important to track because out-of-control discounts and comps can easily sink a healthy restaurant.

The other important items in the sales journal are balance sheet items, like sales tax payable (money you owe the state or local government), gift cards payable receivables (cash you should have received), and credit card deposits you will receive in the future The 4000s are all your income accounts: They record revenue or sales. The debits located in the 4000s are merely those comps or discounts that reduce revenue (and are therefore important to track and keep a close eye on).

The main difference between recording a daily sales journal and other types of sales recordings is that sales are recorded on the day they occur. If you want to dive deep into the financials, have accurate books, or simply just run a great restaurant, the sales journal provides an important blueprint.

TAKE ADVANTAGE OF THE QUICKBOOKS MEMORIZING FEATURE

QuickBooks has great features that allow journal transactions to be memorized. The concept of memorizing transactions in QuickBooks is like an internet browser auto-filling your address into the address section when you make an online purchase. The only nuance related to QuickBooks is that you have to change the dollar values for the memorized transaction. Memorizing the journal entry transaction will help expedite the process of recording your daily sales.

The only part of the sample sales journal offered above that will change when memorizing transactions is account 2300, Gift Cards. In the example offered, a gift card is used for a purchase. It will switch to a credit when you are making a sale of a gift card. Remember that if you sold more gift cards then you received, it will be a credit and vice versa. Let's dive in on where to find this:

PROCESS FOR MEMORIZING TRANSACTIONS

QUICKBOOKS DESKTOP

1) From the home screen, visit the top bar navigation and select Company.
2) When the drop-down appears, select Make General Journal Entries.
3) Once the journal entry screen appears, enter the sales journal as outlined previously in this chapter.
4) Once this is entered properly (I recommend entering 0 for all debit and credits for the memorized transaction), select Memorize in the center middle of the screen.
5) Name the entry (I recommend, "Daily Sales Journal").
6) Select if you would like to be reminded or not, and then select frequency.
7) Click OK: Now the transaction is memorized.

QUICKBOOKS ONLINE

1) From the home screen, select the gear icon located in the top right of the screen.
2) Under Lists, select Recurring Transactions.
3) On the top right of the screen select New.
4) From the option list, select the type of entry you would like to add; for sales entries, select Journal Entry.

5) Complete the template name (I recommend "Daily Sales Journal").

6) Select a schedule, complete the internal start date, and complete the sales journal entry based on the information provided earlier in the chapter.

The above concept works for a multitude of transactions, simply start the process by creating the type of entry you would like to create (invoice, sales receipt, etc.).

TO ACCESS MEMORIZED TRANSACTIONS

QUICKBOOKS DESKTOP

1) From the home screen, visit Lists in the top main navigation.

2) Select Memorized Transaction List from the drop-down.

3) There, select the journal entry you want to use.

4) Enter the data from your POS report into the journal entry.

5) Ensure the entry balances, and then save and close.

QUICKBOOKS ONLINE

1) From the home screen, select the gear icon located in the top right of the screen.

2) Under Lists, select Recurring Transactions.

3) There, the transaction you previously saved as a recurring transaction will be listed.

4) On the right of the screen, select Use to utilize this entry.

5) Enter the data from your POS system and save and close the entry.

Trust me, the legwork you will save in the future makes the work required to set up memorized transactions worth it.

PRO TIP

If today is January 2nd, 2019, I recommend titling the journal entry "sls-01-02-19." This allows you to quickly find an entry for a specific day. When memorizing the transaction, I usually just name this journal entry in memorized sales "Daily Sales Journal."

A JOURNAL ENTRY A DAY

Since you're using the accrual accounting method, each day should get its own journal entry. That means that expenses and revenues for the month will align. How do you know you have all the right sales in the correct month? You will label each daily sales by the date—something like "sls 02-01-19" for February 1, 2019.

HANDLING HOUSE ACCOUNTS

If your restaurant has customers with credit terms, this likely means that those clients are businesses (such as hotels, country clubs, or something similar) and have withstood the scrutiny of a credit check. Unless you know Dave the regular guest really well, I wouldn't recommend extending him credit terms or allowing him to use a house account. At the end of the day, cash is king, and Dave may not always pay.

To best track house account sales, ring them up in the POS system like normal and treat them as regular sales. Add another form of payment to the POS or cash registers, and call it "house account." This should be set up with a manager's password and should be checked daily to ensure that abuse does not occur. This is the best way to track sales that are part of normal business but may be paid at a later date. Your staff will use this house account method of payment when house sales need to be recorded. Having a house account adds an additional reconciliation when checking out the servers at the end of their shift and when closing out the day.

For your back office, the house account transaction gets treated very differently than the rest of the transactions. You treat it as you would a credit card receivable account. It is considered a current asset that will increase as your house account customers increase their tabs. Therefore, you will simply add this liability account to your chart of accounts and debit this account in your sales journal, as shown below:

ACCOUNT	DEBIT	CREDIT
4110 - Lunch Sales		$400
4120 - Dinner Sales		$400
4130 - Food Comps	$50	
4140 - Food Discounts	$50	
4310 - N/A Beverages		$100
4320 - Liquor Sales		$100
4330 - Beer Sales		$100

4350 - Wine Sales		$100
4360 - Beverage Comps	$50	
4370 - Beverage Discounts	$50	
2210 - Sales Tax Payable		$100
2300 - Gift Cards	$100	
2280 - Tips Payable		$200
1000 - Cash On Hand	$100	
1150 - Credit Card Receivable	$500	
1175 - House Account	$600	
Total	$1500	$1500

If catering is a part of your restaurant business pay close attention to the following sections; if not, feel free to skip to the next chapter.

PRO TIP

Before you merely extend credit to a customer you should A) have done a credit check, or B) just not extend credit. I find it good practice for all businesses to take a deposit or full payment for an order in advance. It is fine to sort out the final gratuity amount or chase a bill for the additional services rendered, but always make sure that your fixed costs are covered before rendering services.

CATERING: INVOICING CUSTOMERS

Not all restaurants need to issue invoices. However, restaurant operations that provide in-house catering, office catering, or similar services
typically issue invoices to ensure that payment is received. (Usually, it
is best to send invoices ahead of time and confirm payment before an
event.) Restaurant operations that issue invoices should be aware that
invoicing is an important aspect above and beyond daily sales journals
and should be treated differently than daily sales journals.

CATERING: HANDLING ACCOUNTS RECEIVABLE

A catering operation is a bit different than setting up customers
with access to the restaurant's house account. While a house account
offers customers credit within the current restaurant establishment, a
catering operation is an entirely different business from the restaurant
and has its own sales component. Consequently, these businesses to
which your catering services are sold should be treated as receivables,
invoiced ahead of time, and tracked a bit differently. QuickBooks
Online and QuickBooks Desktop can handle this invoicing aspect for
your business. You will track these like normal accounts receivable,
depositing the receivables as in the standard account receivable function in QuickBooks. Let's take a look at how this works.

CATERING: SETTING UP ITEMS

In the realm of QuickBooks, specific catering items are set up as
noninventory items. Though there is an option to track these as
inventory items, as I will cover later in this book, the suggested
methodology that is most efficient for tracking inventory is one
that is not tracked within the QuickBooks inventory system.

Knowing how the catering business performs relative to other revenue centers will allow for optimization of your business. I recommend tracking catering sales separately from daily restaurant sales on the income statement. Refer to the previous chapter where you outlined the chart of accounts and 4500 referred to catering. You will take this and expand as follows:

• •

4510 - Catering Food Sales

4520 - Catering Beverage Sales

4530 - Catering Service Fee

4540 - Catering Comps

4550 - Catering Discounts

• •

Once you have your income chart of accounts set up for tracking catering, you can then add the necessary pieces to record sales in an invoice format. But first you will need to set up some QuickBooks items:

Setting up items is a basic aspect of properly invoicing customers. Certain items should show up certain ways: Some should increase income, some should decrease, and so on.

QUICKBOOKS DESKTOP

1) From the home screen, visit Lists from the top navigation bar.
2) Select Item List from the drop-down—this will open all of your previously generated items.
3) To create a new item, you simply go to the bottom left of the screen and select Item button and New from the

pop-up menu.

4) From here, enter the product as a service from the drop-down.

5) Provide the item name, price, and additional details (note that you can always modify these later if necessary).

6) Map the item to your chart of accounts general ledger code as explained above.

7) Save and close the item.

You now have items set up within your system to properly track your catering business. This section has walked you through creating a generalized item, such as catering food sales and catering food beverages. For a low volume business or for one where additional collateral is provided, this system will work for you. For more complex or potentially more discerning customers, I recommend providing more granular details.

For example, for a restaurant that caters large corporate events, having items prepopulated will save time on the sales process. Let's take a popular dessert item like cookies. These are sold by the dozen and have a preset price. It is most efficient to create a unique item for this within QuickBooks. For example, instead of creating a catering food sales item, you would generate a 12-Dozen Chocolate Chip Cookies item with a fixed price. Following the above steps and creating a noninventory item and related price will expedite the time it takes to create and invoice customers in your catering operation.

QUICKBOOKS ONLINE

The online setup is similar to the desktop setup. Though the user interface is quite different, the concept of setting up noninventory items that are services still holds true.

1) From the home page, select the gear icon located in the top right.

2) Under the gear icon, you will find an item called Products and Services located under the Lists column.

3) Once you access this, you can set up a new item by simply clicking New.

4) After this sheet populates, you will select the service item. (This is a noninventory tracked item, though you actually do track inventory. Because you're going to track it a bit differently than in the QuickBooks sense of inventory tracking, ignore selecting the inventory option for now.)

5) You want to generate a name that is similar to the chart of accounts. For example, "catering food sales" chart of account-related items should be "catering food sales" items and similar for other items.

6) No SKU or category or set price is necessary, and the income account code should match the general ledger code you referenced previously—i.e., the catering food sales item should be 4510.

Repeat for all chart of accounts items. Now you have items set up within your QuickBooks system to properly track your catering business. You can now proceed with invoicing that catering client!

- -

PRO TIP

A handy trick in QuickBooks Desktop is simply right-clicking a preexisting item to duplicate it. When you right-click, most of your settings are retained and you merely have to change the name and GL account.

- -

INVOICE CUSTOMERS

Though this process may seem quite simple, it's best I walk through it again just in case. Assuming you have set up your items as outlined above, you are good to proceed to this step. It is a simple process but important that you follow the correct steps outlined below:

1) Create the invoice.
2) Fill out the invoice with all the pertinent information.
3) Send the invoice.

CREATE INVOICE

Most restaurant owners who also run catering businesses use a similar system for knowing which customers have purchased and will receive which items: Typically, once an order is made, a banquet event order (BEO) is generated by the sales staff to notify the kitchen and accounting department about what will be served and what should be billed. Once this handy information is made available, you can then create an invoice. To do this, simply select the customer you would like to invoice under Customers, if they are a repeat customer. If they are not a repeat customer, you will need to generate a new customer within QuickBooks.

Below follows step-by-step instructions for generating an invoice.

QUICKBOOKS DESKTOP, STEP 1

1) From the home screen, select Create Invoices from the middle left of the screen, or visit the top navigation bar titled Customers. (When invoicing a new customer, select Customers from the top navigation, then select Customer Center, and then choose New Customer & Job from the top left of the screen).
2) If you elected to use the top bar navigation to access

invoices, you then need to select Create Invoices.

3) Once you are on the Invoice page, you will continue to Step 2 below.

QUICKBOOKS ONLINE, STEP 1

1) From the home screen, select the plus icon located in the top right of the screen. (For those of you who need to add a new customer, simply visit Sales on the left main navigation bar; then select New Customer from the top right).

2) Once the additional popup appears, under Customers, select Invoice, then proceed to Step 2 below.

Once you've generated your invoice you must complete it by filling out the invoice with all pertinent information

QUICKBOOKS DESKTOP STEP 2

1) Enter the customer's name in the top left.

2) Next, enter the date, invoice number, and purchase order number (if necessary).

3) The Bill To, Ship To, and Terms should appear based on your previously entered information for this vendor.

4) Next, enter your item code based on your previously created items (for example, catering food sales).

5) Enter the quantity, change the description if necessary, and verify the pricing.

6) To complete, simply select save and close.

QUICKBOOKS ONLINE STEP 2

1) Enter the customer's name in the top left.

2) Next, enter the date and invoice number.

3) The Billing Address, Terms, and Due Date should be based on the previously entered vendor specific information.

4) Next, enter your item code based on your previously created items (for example, catering food sales).

5) Enter the quantity, and change the description and rate if necessary.

6) To complete, simply save and close the invoice.

PRO TIP

For those looking to keep accrual-based books, (accounting records that match revenue to expenses, which is my recommended approach), set the invoice date to the date of the event. Even if you received payments such as deposits in advance, you can simply apply that payment to the future invoice or create a prepaid events asset on your chart of accounts. Journal this to accounts receivable and reference the correct customer during the time of their event—then you can use this credit to pay the deposit of the invoice in the correct period.

Once you complete the above steps, QuickBooks will automatically generate the invoice number. It's therefore usually best to leave the invoice number field alone. That said, some organizations will have a per-customer system, so do feel free to change if necessary.

When filling out the sales information, use the items you created earlier in this chapter. Remember that you can use an item like catering food sales and change the description to match what was actually ordered.

I always recommend double-checking over your invoice before saving. You want to ensure that your item count and rates look correct; additionally, you want to ensure your total is relative to your expectations.

SEND THE INVOICE
Sending invoices via QuickBooks is fairly straightforward, but worth reiterating.

QUICKBOOKS DESKTOP
Once the invoice information has been entered as outlined above, from the top of the invoice screen, simply select Print or Email. If printed, you have the option to either print a physical copy or print to a pdf to send later. The email option sends to the default email or allows you to enter an email if none is on file.

QUICKBOOKS ONLINE
To send an invoice, simply select save and send when entering the invoice information as outlined above. The other option is to print to a pdf and send out as an email attachment. Find the method that works best for your team and run with it.

RECEIVING PAYMENTS
Those who run a catering operation or who invoice customers directly will need to receive payments. (If you use journal entries to record daily sales, skip this section.)

If you created an invoice in QuickBooks to record a sale to a customer, at some point you expect to receive payment related to that invoice. Receiving payments is only necessary if you have an open invoice to apply the payment to.

Most owners will receive money to close an open invoice. However, owners will sometimes receive money when an invoice hasn't been created. This occurs in the off chance that a customer made a last-minute order that did not go through the standard sales process. If you receive a payment from a customer and you have not created an invoice in QuickBooks, then you need to generate a sales receipt related to that customer to process the payment.

Let's take a look at the steps needed to properly process customer payments:

1) Receive payment.
2) Enter customer payment.
3) Confirm payment was applied.

RECEIVE PAYMENT

I recommend having the check, credit card payment, or wire information in front of you. This will ensure you have the correct dollar amounts and that the proper invoices are referenced.

Remember, double checking this information now will not only make the next few steps easier, it will make the entire monthly close process simpler.

ENTER CUSTOMER PAYMENT

Entering the customer payment has quite a few components, and it is very important that you get them correct. These can range from the vendor names, invoice numbers, dollar amounts, and dates the receivable was processed. Not handling the following items correctly will result in both incorrect accounts payable, statements, messed up bank balances and many more headaches.

FOR DESKTOP USERS

For Desktop customers the above steps are very similar except for two additional steps: receiving payments under the customer section, and making the deposit under banking. Owners who receive numerous deposits daily should ensure that they make a single deposit with multiple customer payment receipts. This will make sure that banking goes smoothly.

1) From the home screen, select Receive Payments from the middle of the screen, or select Customers from the top navigation.
2) Select Receive Payments if you started from the top-level navigation.
3) Enter the Received From, which is the customer who remitted payment.
4) The invoices related to that customer will then populate the screen.
5) Select the invoices made with the relative payment.
6) Then ensure that the date, check (or reference) number, and payment type are correct.
7) Select save and close in the bottom right of the screen.

For QuickBooks Desktop users, complete the above steps until all payments have been processed. Then, make deposits within QuickBooks.

1) From the home screen, select Record Deposits from the right side of the screen, or select Banking from the top navigation.
2) Then, select Make Deposits if you started from the top-level navigation.
3) Select the items to be included in this deposit from the pop-up; then select OK.
4) Ensure the account, date, and memo match your records.

5) Verify that the amounts and items included in the deposit match your physical deposit.

6) Then select save and close.

FOR ONLINE USERS

1) From the home screen, select the plus icon located in the top right.

2) Select Receive Payments located under Customers.

3) Then select the correct customer's name from the drop-down.

4) After that, select the payment date, which should be the date that you received payment.

5) After that, select the payment method from the drop-down list (options are check, cash, or credit card).

6) Ensure your proper bank account has been selected (change if necessary).

7) Add a memo if you would like to add a note for future reference.

8) Finally, save and close this transaction.

. . . .

PRO TIP

If you are depositing multiple payments in a given day in QuickBooks Online, you can either deposit each item into undeposited funds and then deposit them all into the bank account or deposit each individually into the bank account and then match all those deposits to the one deposit that clears your bank account under the banking section.

. . . .

CONFIRM PAYMENT

The last step confirms you applied the payment correctly. To do this, enter the customer section of QuickBooks; visit the customer you just referenced above, and ensure the invoice you received payment for is marked as paid within the system.

CONCLUSION

In this chapter, I covered the main components of recording sales, inputting sales journal entries, and invoicing for catering houses. Most readers will likely not be providing catering services and I recommend spending the time to create memorized transactions, as these will serve as time savers in the future. Though journal entries may seem overwhelming at first, the sales journal entries for restaurants ensure that you are capturing all your revenue types from all your different revenue streams. No longer will you be unsure about the food and beverage portions of your sales; no longer will you simply record cash as it is deposited (yikes, what was your cash shortfall?). My daily sales method utilizing sales journal entries will help you become a better restaurant manager and owner.

6

MANAGING
DAY-TO-DAY LIABILITIES
(TIPS AND SALES TAX)

MONEY OWED

Liabilities are one of the main focuses of small business accounting (think accounting equation, if you want to get technical). Similarly, they are the main components of operating a business. This chapter helps you ensure that liabilities of all types are properly recorded and tracked. While the chapter may seem all-encompassing, I've tried to ensure that all liability-related items fall here (all except payroll and accounts payable, which merit their own chapters).

EVERYONE OWES SOMEONE *(But Restaurants Owe More)*

Why are liabilities more important for restaurants than most other small businesses? The reason is simple: Restaurant liabilities— from sales tax to vendor payments—occur multiple times a week, if not daily. Most other small businesses, even if they operate at the scale of a small- to midsize restaurant, order products or services and receive deliveries weekly or monthly. Meanwhile, restaurants at decent scale have multiple delivery trucks coming daily and varying services provided on the regular. The fact that the scope of liabilities is so large makes it all the more important to understand and track them correctly.

No matter how big and successful your business gets, at some point, you will owe someone something. This could be your annual tax bill or your monthly sales tax. This chapter covers the restaurant nuances related to who and what you owe.

Payroll tips and sales tax (formerly known as accounts payable) can be confusing topics. They involve paying other people at the correct time and for the correct amount. Getting it right is more science than art, but this book will bring people who are new to the world of liabilities up to speed quickly.

For most restaurants, major liabilities—or, the categories in which restaurants owe money—include tips, sales tax, short-term debt, long-term debt, and accounts payable. In this chapter, I will discuss tips and sales tax in more depth.

TIPS DEFINED

What exactly are tips? Tips or gratuities are defined by *Merriam Webster* as "something given voluntarily or beyond obligation usually for some service." Tips or gratuities are simply money given by choice on top of a bill or invoice and not considered part of the sale. There is often a lot of confusion around what is considered tips versus restaurant income, so it is important for all restaurant owners to ensure they are compliant with local statutes.

Tips are very important in the hospitality world. Both you and I may agree with the above definition of gratuities, but most individuals working within the world of hospitality do not define tips as voluntary. Tips are usually expected, and they're usually expected to be between 15 to 20 percent.

Since tips are inherently different than the bill or invoice, it makes sense that the accounting for these items is different as well. You are going to track tips via journal entries on both the sales side and payroll side. These tips live on the balance sheet and are reflected as a current liability. Confused already? Don't fret, more details to come in this chapter!

The nuances of tips can be a bit confusing, but it's important that you understand that tips are simply money flowing into the business that is not yours. You may collect tips in a number of different or combined ways: You may only collect credit card tips; you may collect cash and credit card tips; your employees may take their cash home. Whatever amount of money you collect that is defined as tips are monies you are holding in trust for someone else.

TIPS ARE NOT REVENUE

As you probably learned from the earlier chapter on recording restaurant sales, tips were not included in top line sales. They are instead included in the cash and credit card received and treated as a liability to be paid out.

Tips are a balance sheet item. That means they should not appear on the income statement at all. They should not be included in top line sales. They should not be included as an expense under payroll. Think: Tips are a liability—meaning, they are being held for the future.

Revenue or sales refers to the revenues earned when a company sells its goods, products, merchandise, etc. For restaurant owners, restaurant revenue accrues when you sell food, drinks, accoutrements, etc. Tips are not revenue or sales.

PAYROLL TIPS

These tips are generally associated with payroll. This means they are associated with a paycheck, end up on a paycheck, or are accounted for on a paycheck. They generally operate in two different forms: inflows and outflows. The manner they inflow varies from business to business and according to how a business is structured.

INFLOWS

Tips tend to flow into the business daily (hint: they're one of the reasons I strongly recommend accounting for sales daily, as outlined in the previous chapter). Tips tend to flow into the business both in a cash format and from your payment processer. For example, a customer can add a tip to their credit card bill, or they can leave cash on top of either a credit card bill or a cash tab.

One of the keys to accounting for tips is ensuring that you track them for both cash sales and credit card sales. If you simply account for tips on credit card sales, you are underreporting the tips on cash sales. Make sure you track these as it is your responsibility to report this to the IRS on behalf of your employees. Make sure you adjust how you remit payment to them or account for cash tips to ensure that you track these figures correctly.

OUTFLOWS

In the world of restaurants, money seems to come in and leave shortly thereafter. The tips come in and are held in trust for your employees and then remitted to them on payday.

There are a few options for distributing tips. One, an employee is allowed to take all their tips home on the day they work. Two, an employee is allowed to take all cash tips home on the day they work. Third, employees are not allowed to take any tips home.

It is my recommendation that you choose option two. I understand that we all want our money as soon as possible. However, what many restaurant owners fail to realize is that by going with option one, you are serving as a bank to your employees—essentially loaning them money that you do not have yet. Remember, you won't get your credit card settlements for two to three days after they are processed.

TIPS OR SERVICE CHARGES?

Most people assume (even some restaurant owners assume) that the gratuity or tip that is defined on the receipt as "automatic gratuity of 18 percent for a large party" is a tip for the server. In reality, depending on the establishment, it's possible that none, some, or all of that money will go to the server. Tips and service charges are reported differently on payroll reports and in restaurant accounting. According to the IRS, in order to determine if a payment is treated as a tip, these four factors must be considered:

1) The payment must be made free from compulsion;
2) The customer must have the unrestricted right to determine the amount;
3) The payment should not be the subject of negotiations or dictated by employer policy; and
4) Generally, the customer has the right to determine who receives the payment.

If these factors do not justify the payment being treated as a tip, it is treated as a service charge. So, the compulsory tip defined on the bottom of the receipt actually makes it a service charge, and the restaurant can therefore treat it differently.

How you treat service charges is up to you and your team. However, I always recommend that before you pinch pennies, you focus on the right ones to pinch. In layman's terms, that means before you start keeping some of the service fees or even splitting them, you consider renegotiating with your food vendors and renegotiating your product or laundry services. I always find that a happy team makes life easier.

• •

PRO TIP

Service fees are usually considered revenue. However, this really depends on the state you operate within and how that state defines service fees. Certain states may even require that you collect and pay sales taxes on these monies.

• •

TIP REPORTING REQUIREMENTS

Obviously, you are a restaurant owner, restaurant bookkeeper, or an accountant. It is your responsibility as the steward of the restaurant's funds to understand that employee tips are your concern. Gratuities are income, and it's your responsibility to properly report your employees' wages.

Did you know that when employees fail to pay taxes on their tips the IRS considers this a form of tax evasion? Yes, failing to pay taxes on tips is technically breaking the law. Unreported tips will also cause an employee's W-2 income to be lower than it actually is. Unreported income can become a problem when the employee applies for a car loan or a house loan and finds out their income is too low to qualify.

The restaurant can quickly become liable if it helps the employee under-report tips. In case of an audit, an auditor will quickly find if tips have been reported or not. It is important for the restaurant to require employees to report all of their tips, or the restaurant runs the risk of incurring additional taxes and penalties for failing to report and tax the tips.

Luckily, it is easy to report and track credit card tips with a simple report run at the end of every day. Think POS daily report! This report will have your receivable amounts from all your credit card processors, including cash sales! It is just as simple to report this on employee paychecks.

Getting employees to report their cash tips is easy as well, and usually depends on setting the appropriate corporate culture from the top. It is the employee's responsibility to report the amount of cash and credit card tips received to the employer. It is not the employer's responsibility to keep track of the tips collected by each employee. While the employer may know how much a particular server collected in credit card tips, the employer has no way of knowing how much cash a server picked up off the tables, nor does the employer know the number of tips that the server shared with the busser or the bartender.

EDUCATE YOUR TEAM AND BE TRANSPARENT ABOUT TIPS

There are many different ways to manage tips. Whichever way works for you and your team, you can make the process easier by creating a straightforward and transparent policy for your entire staff to follow.

An effective tip policy will match your specific business needs and will work with the tools you have at your disposal, such as the gratuity tracking features in your POS systems. Employees need to understand this policy, and they need to buy in.

Once you form a gratuity policy, I recommend that you document and distribute it to each staff member when they're hired. It should clearly outline your restaurant's process for handling tips and how employees are expected to report the gratuities they collect.

For your employees' benefit, your policy should include a grievance process in case problems do occur. Having a transparent policy that you share with your employees when they're hired will help build an all-star team from day one and prevent problems. For an industry fraught with poor HR, as the restaurant industry is, it's helpful to get ahead of any pushback before it occurs.

SALES TAX

Restaurant owners owe tips, but they also owe sales tax. Sales tax is a tax paid to the governing body for the sale of certain goods and services. Most transactions in a restaurant include products that fall under these goods and services. There are nuances that vary state to state (for example, service fees are sometimes taxed or not; to-go items may be treated differently; etc.). Look into any nuances for your state, but always err on the side of caution.

SALES TAX OFFICER

As a restaurant owner, you serve as a revenue collection agent for the government. That's right—you are tasked with collecting the monies the government says is theirs. As with tips, you are a steward of these funds, but unfortunately cannot do as you please with them. You must collect, keep a close eye on, and remit these monies to the government within the proper time window.

PRO TIP

Remember, sales tax is levied on the final customer. This is why your vendors do not tax the goods they sell you: You are not the final customer of that bulk order of Marzano tomatoes—Joe at the bar who ordered the red sauce is!

DOES MY RESTAURANT HAVE TO PAY SALES TAX?

Does a chef cook? Nice try, but of course! I have yet to work with a restaurant that does not pay sales tax. Like any other business, you are required to pay sales tax if you have nexus in a state (soon the rules will change and become stricter in order to target online retailers). So, if your restaurant has a brick and mortar location, also known as a building (or even a food truck), you will definitely need to pay sales tax.

HOW DO I PAY SALES TAX?

Sales tax payment options and dates vary from state to state. Additionally, the requirements change depending on the size of your business, which is determined not by how many employees you have, but by how much product you sell on a monthly basis.

For example, let's take a look at New York State. Prior to getting to the point where you can make a sale in your restaurant, you must apply with the state to get approved to collect sales tax on their behalf. Once that process is complete, and you have been approved, then you can start collecting sales tax.

Sales tax payments often occur a few weeks after the end of the previous month. For February, the sales tax payment would be due in late to mid-March of the same year. I recommend keeping an eye on the dollar amount of this liability, the date, and your ability to cover this expense. As you know, when it comes to sales tax, you are only holding money for the government. The government will get its money no matter what, and if that means shutting down your place, that's what will happen.

NEW YORK 2019 PART-QUARTERLY (MONTHLY) FILING DUE DATES
For sellers who have been assigned to the part-quarterly (monthly) filing frequency, the New York Department of Taxation and Finance has set the following filing deadlines for 2019 sales and use tax returns:

TAX COLLECTION PERIOD	FILING DEADLINE
January	February 20, 2019
February	March 20, 2019
March	April 20, 2019
April	May 21, 2019
May	June 20, 2019
June	July 20, 2019
July	August 20, 2019
August	September 20, 2019
September	October 22, 2019
October	November 20, 2019
November	December 20, 2019
December	January 22, 2020

As you see above, even for tax payers who file on a monthly basis, some time is allotted to get your books in order and verify the amounts due. Remember, monthly filers are usually based on dollar amounts or some other criteria. My assumption is that just as it happens in New York State, if you operate a business and qualify for monthly prepayments in another state, you will be notified. Of course, please do not take my word on this—consult a local CPA.

NEW YORK 2019 QUARTERLY FILING DUE DATES

The New York Department of Revenue defines quarters starting in March of each year (note months for each quarter in the table below). For sellers who have been assigned to the quarterly filing frequency, the New York Department of Taxation and Finance has set the following filing deadlines for 2019 sales and use tax returns:

TAX COLLECTION PERIOD	FILING DEADLINE
Q1 (March – May)	June 20, 2019
Q2 (June – August)	September 20, 2019
Q3 (September – November)	December 20, 2019
Q4 (December – February)	March 20, 2020

As you see above, quarterly filers get a bit more time to get their reporting in order. Similar to the monthly filers, you get about 20 days until quarter-end to complete and perform your tax filing.

NEW YORK 2019 ANNUAL FILING DUE DATES

For filers who have been assigned to the annual filing frequency, the New York Department of Taxation and Finance has set the following filing deadlines for 2019 sales and use tax returns:

TAX COLLECTION PERIOD	FILING DEADLINE
2019 (Months vary for some states)	March 20, 2020

It is unlikely that you sell such a small amount that you qualify for an annual filing. Though, as I have stated previously, be sure to consult your local CPA or sales tax representative.

Smart restaurant owners like you educate themselves: Oftentimes, at least in New York State, owners fail to realize that the monthly filing is a prepayment of the quarterly taxes. This means that both monthly deposits and quarterly filings are due—double the work! Consult your local CPA or tax department to verify your responsibilities.

PRO TIP

Sales tax money is never yours to use for the operations of the business. Too many times, I have seen owners use sales tax money for payroll expenses, resulting—predictably—in cash flow problems that can equate to the closure of the business. Avoid this from day one by setting up a savings account specifically for sales tax received, and transfer the amount received weekly into this account to make your monthly or quarterly payments.

ACCOUNTING FOR SALES TAX

For many new business owners, sales tax is conceptually a bit challenging to understand. It is money received that is not yours and that is not income. It is money paid out that is not yours and that is not an expense.

Sales tax is money in trust for the government. It essentially sits on the balance sheet, accruing no interest income or expenses until it is remitted to the government.

Most accountants and bookkeepers have trouble recording the sales tax inflow and often characterize it incorrectly as income. Sales tax is not income! Sales tax is a liability. That is why I suggest in Chapter 5 that you set up sales tax to reflect on the balance sheet.

You do not want sales tax to affect your revenue or income. Sales tax should always tie to the POS. This means the exact amount collected in July, denoted on the balance sheet in the liability accounts, should match the amount paid to the government (unless you get a credit for early payment) for July, usually paid in the following month.

Even though sales tax figures can be pulled directly from the POS system at the end of every month, it is important to validate the information based on your local sales tax statutes. For example, perhaps you rented out tables and chairs for an event, and they were not set up as taxable in your POS, even though they are in fact taxable. By simply exporting the data from your income statement and making the sales tax calculation in Excel, you can verify that you collected all necessary funds and will make payment per local guidelines.

Let's dive a bit deeper into the method for validating your sales tax:

1) Verify that all sales for the period are entered into QuickBooks via journal entries.
2) Reconcile said sales against the POS system, and ensure the amounts are accurate.
3) Review the balance sheet sales tax amounts, and ensure

that it matches the POS system for the period.

4) Export the income statement for the reporting period into Excel.

5) Take the net or gross sales, depending on your sales tax statutes, and calculate this by the appropriate sales tax amounts.

6) Ensure that the amounts from steps 2, 3 and 5 match.

7) If these items do not match, investigate the errors and resolve.

SALES TAX IS NOT REVENUE

Because I see it all too often, let me reiterate: Sales tax is not revenue. It should not show up on your income statement.

Yes, it may be technically part of your cash deposit or credit card deposit, but luckily, you set up your sales journal entry to account for this. You know exactly how much you are receiving in both cash and credit cards, how much of that is sales tax due to the government, and how much is tips payable.

Please, for the sake of my sanity, do not record sales tax as revenue.

SALES TAX IS NOT AN EXPENSE *(with One Exception)*

Yep—sales tax is not an expense, and it should never appear on the income statement. There is one exclusion to this, however.

The only time that sales tax will be an expense is if you incorrectly set up sales tax in your POS system. This means that you collected less monies than you should have. Part of filing sales tax is ensuring that your POS has collected the correct withheld money. Sometimes this does not happen, and to balance the liability account, you must book the expense.

Ultimately, the taxable items were sold regardless of whether or not you set up your system properly, and in most states, this means you owe sales tax monies on these sales. This is the only time that sales tax becomes an expense: You collected $100 in sales tax payable, but you actually owe $125. The difference between what is due and what is collected is the sales tax expense, the $25.

CONCLUSION

Payables of all types can sink your restaurant in the blink of an eye. This entire chapter was devoted to tips payable and sales tax payable for one simple reason, you cannot manage what you do not know. So knowing your restaurant liabilities, in particular the money such as sales tax that you are simply holding for the government and when those funds are due, will result in your ability to better manage those liabilities. By properly managing your day-to-day liabilities, your restaurant will be able to survive both the good times and bad.

PAYROLL

PAYROLL

Payroll is simply the wages paid to both full- and part-time staff members. In exchange for these wages, the restaurant and business receive services. In its basic format, wages are fairly simple, x hours at a y rate result in a paycheck of x times y. If only it were that simple in the world of restaurants!

RESTAURANT PAYROLL

Like the many things this book covers, restaurant payroll is a bit more complex than payroll for other small businesses. Why? Simply put, a majority of the earnings for the staff comes in the form of tips, which are often received by the restaurant and redistributed by the restaurant, adding an entire additional layer of complexity. On top of that, the manager of the business, who typically has only limited human resources experience, is the human resources expert in a world where slip and falls happen all too often. Now, that being said, this chapter has a simple goal, to help you clean up your payroll related accounting, understand that tips aren't revenue nor expenses, and expedite the accounting aspect of payroll.

RESTAURANT SUCCESS

Over the past few years, I have had the privilege of working with many restaurants, as well as with owners, managers, and other team members. I've noticed that the difference between a successful restaurant enterprise and a failing one is actually pretty simple to diagnose.

Obviously, there are lots of factors involved in the success of a great restaurant; meanwhile, lots of little overlooked details can contribute to a restaurant's failure. The biggest drivers of success are ownership and management knowing and understanding their three prime costs: (1) The total of beverage cost of goods, combined with (2) the food cost of goods, and added to (3) labor costs.

Total COGS + Total Labor = Prime Costs

Successful restaurant owners and operators know and understand their prime costs. They establish realistic expectations for these prime costs, budget around them, and push their team to achieve them.

This chapter will explore the labor aspect of the prime cost equation. Since each restaurant is unique, I won't dive into the correct configuration of staffing or management of the clock, but I will help you properly account and implement a better system to track it.

PAYROLL IS A HEADACHE

Every restaurant owner or operator knows that payroll is a giant headache. It is first and foremost the only bill that comes every single week that cannot be paid late. Try telling your employees that you are paying them not on Monday, as you have for the last six months, but later in the week instead. You might end up losing most if not all of your employees, and the Department of Labor will surely be calling you on the phone.

Most accountants and bookkeepers struggle with entering and tracking gross payroll along with net checks. Often, it just seems easier to clear the multiple withdrawals from the payroll company as payroll expenses. Unfortunately, this typically results in misrepresented payroll numbers on the income statement. Some of the charges are wages, some are tips, some are employer taxes, and others are employee taxes. Without separating them out properly, you risk misrepresenting company expenses.

Additionally, payroll expenses are often entered the day a staff member has time to enter them or the day the weekly checks are cut. This almost always results in expenses skewed over multiple periods.

In the rest of this chapter, I will help you set up a proper payroll journal, properly account for net checks and taxes, and correctly recognize expenses in the proper period.

USE A FULL-SERVICE PAYROLL PROVIDER

Yes, being a frugal business owner is important. Wasteful spending results in income statements that show negative numbers. Most small business owners can agree on that.

However, there is a huge difference between being frugal and being cheap. In the service of frugality, I recommend using a full-service payroll provider. Managing weekly payables is challenging enough before worrying about making all the correct weekly, monthly, and quarterly tax payments to the correct departments.

Pay the extra money on a monthly basis, and ensure that your employees' wages are compliant, their tax rates are correct, and you are compliant with all the payroll tax departments.

Some of these full-service payroll providers even offer workman's compensation based on the overall payroll expense. That's right— it is removed simply and cleanly every week along with the rest of your payroll expense.

There are two main full-service payroll providers: ADP and Gusto. Both offer the necessary services for small and growing restaurants. Comparing the two products is beyond the scope of this book, but

I recommend you use one of them. The remainder of this chapter will show you how to account for these full-service providers and ensure the correct setup of these accounting entries.

PROPER EXPENSE RECOGNITION

Under accrual-based accounting, revenues and expenses should match. But what does that even mean? Well, with regards to payroll, it means that when you create journal entries for the sales, the correlated payroll journal entry should be on the income statement for the similar period.

For example, if you are reviewing last week's performance, you run a report from Monday through Sunday. Assuming that your payroll runs from Monday to Sunday, within that report, you should have seven sales journal entries and one associated payroll entry. To run this report in QuickBooks Desktop, visit Reports at the top of the screen, and select Company and Financial from the drop-down menu; then select Profit and Loss Statement. Next, modify the dates for the period in question.

To run this report in QuickBooks Online, simply log in to your home screen, visit the Reports section on the left side of the screen. From there, select Profit and Loss from the Business Overview section. The key here is to modify the time range at the top of the report to the preferred dates.

Understanding that labor for one period is associated with sales for that same period is proper business management and also proper accounting.

That is why properly entering sales journal entries, discussed in Chapter 5, is so fundamental!

As I recommended earlier in the chapter, you should use a third party to manage your payroll—it's just easier. That said, you will also enter a journal entry on a weekly basis (covered in the upcoming sections). Before I dive into how to create these journal entries, you should understand that the journal entry should hit or impact the income statement for the period the wages were actually earned.

So, even though payroll may come out of your bank account a week or two weeks later. Proper business management and accounting means that the payroll journal entry should be entered in the week the services were performed.

For example, for the services rendered by employees in the first week of November, journal entries should be entered the last day the employee services were performed. This correlates the sales and the expenses properly for the period.

UNDERSTANDING TIPS PAYABLE FOR PAYROLL

As the restaurant owner or manager, you can decide how you would like to structure your nightly tip-out. Some restaurants prefer to let their employees take home cash tips and credit card tips, while others prefer to let employees take home only cash tips. I mentioned this earlier in the book, but I strongly recommend the latter as it usually takes three to four days for credit card transactions to clear a bank account, and floating money that you do not have yet is bad business practice.

There are two ways to account for tips payable: including or not including the cash tips. Therefore, the exact configuration of your payroll journals depends on whether you account for cash tips payable by including or not including them. The following section will guide you through the payroll journal entry under the assumption that tips payable has been recorded on the balance sheet, per the previous chapter. So, the next example is based on a restaurant paying out cash tips at the end of the night and paying out credit card tips after they are received on the payroll for the period. This is the restaurant policy I most readily see, though this will certainly change as we move toward a cashless restaurant world.

PAYROLL JOURNAL COMPONENTS

The payroll journal is one of the most popular journal entries within the world of accounting. Payroll is often a complex transaction with many moving parts, and the journal entry seamlessly captures all this accounting activity. Despite the fact that it is extremely common, it can be a bit complex, even for an experienced bookkeeper or business owner.

Some of the items I am about to cover are not simply QuickBooks specific, but relate to the basic accounting for payroll and payroll related items. Pay attention: This information will be very valuable in your weekly or biweekly processing of payroll.

The payroll journal entry consists of a few main aspects outlined below:

GROSS WAGES
This is the portion of your payroll expense paid to your staff and is often broken up by departments, such as FOH management, BOH management, and general management.

BONUS EXPENSE
Ever have a great month and given a bonus to your hard-working staff? Or, do you give an annual or quarterly bonus (think holiday

or a performance related bonus)? You'll record this information under this additional expense line item.

PAYROLL TAX EXPENSE

A portion of the taxes paid for payroll are an expense of the company, and a portion are a contribution from your employees. This line item indicates the amount that your restaurant contributes to taxes, including social security, Medicare, and unemployment insurance. Since not all taxes paid to the government are the company's expenses, this line item tracks the company's expense.

BENEFIT CONTRA ACCOUNT

If your employees contribute to a benefit program, this is where you will account for this. For example, do you provide health insurance? Well, part of that is your expense and part of it is your employees' expense.

PAYROLL CLEARING ACCOUNT (NET CHECK ACCOUNT)

Some employers still pay via check (I recommend direct deposit because it is much quicker, and I hope by now you know that time is money). This account is where those net check amounts are recorded to clear in the future. For example, when John gets his weekly check, you clear part of the journal entry into the account showing the monies are due and then issue a net check for his paycheck.

WAGE WITHDRAWAL

When you use a full-service provider, they often make a few withdrawals for each pay period to help with accounting. One of those main withdrawals is the wage expense that is debited from your bank account. This bank withdrawal usually states "net wages" or similar on the bank transaction detail, and the portion of the journal entry for this should match the withdrawal specifically.

TAX WITHDRAWAL

When you use a full-service provider, it often makes a few withdrawals for each pay period to help with accounting. One of those main withdrawals is for the tax expense. The tax expenses include both the employee and employer tax expense, meaning it is a tax that both the employee and the employer pay. This comes out in one withdrawal and usually denotes "taxes" or "tax payment" in the withdrawal.

TIPS PAYABLE

As I've mentioned before and will mention again, tips are not an expense for your business, they are simply a pass-through that needs to be recorded as earned wages for your employees. These pass-through entries live on the balance sheet for a short time, and then are zeroed out when a counter-transaction is made. Sometimes tips are paid on checks, and sometimes they are paid out in cash nightly; either way, they need to be accounted for.

PRO TIP

Tips payable is one of the most confusing concepts of the restaurant payroll journal. If entered incorrectly, it will cause your payroll journal to not balance. The best way to understand this is to understand that if your employees have already earned tips payable (in most cases), it is not an expense for your restaurant, but is instead taxable income for the employees (and simply a pass-through for your restaurant).

PAYROLL JOURNAL ENTRY

Below is an example of a restaurant journal entry.

Of course, this is simply an example, and depending on the addition or removal of specific items, your journal entry may look different. For example, if you run an events venue, you may have a service charge that you need to account for that you treat differently than tips payable. In fact, you may treat that service charge as an expense because you are in a state where you need to pay sales tax on it.

The following example assumes all employees are on direct deposit.

Date: 09/30/2019		
ACCOUNT NAME	**DEBIT**	**CREDIT**
6011 - Gross Wages - Management FOH	$5,000	
6012 - Gross Wages - FOH Hourly	$2,500	
6021 - Gross Wage - BOH Management	$2,500	
6022 - Gross Wages - BOH Hourly	$2,500	
6065 - Payroll Tax Expense	$3,000	
2280 - Tips Payable	$2,500	
1010 - Wage Withdrawal Bank Account		$12,500
1010 - Tax Withdrawal Bank Account		$5,500
Total	$18,000	$18,000

The following example assumes employees are split between direct deposit and manual checks.

Date: 09/30/2019		
ACCOUNT NAME	DEBIT	CREDIT
6011 - Gross Wages - Management FOH	$5,000	
6012 - Gross Wages - FOH Hourly	$2,500	
6021 - Gross Wage - BOH Management	$5,000	
6022 - Gross Wages - BOH Hourly	$2,500	
6065 - Payroll Tax Expense	$3,000	
2280 - Tips Payable	$2,500	
1010 - Wage Withdrawal Bank Account		$8,500
1010 - Tax Withdrawal Bank Account		$6,500
2220 - Net Checks - To Clear Later		$5,500
Total	$20,500	$20,500

Please note that you can break up departments as you see fit. For example, those with large BOH management, FOH management, and administrative staff may want to include all three of those accounts, while small restaurants or cafés may prefer only one line item for management.

UNDERSTANDING NET CHECKS

Some employees in the restaurant industry prefer to receive a physical paycheck on a weekly or biweekly basis. This is a normal request and should be accommodated, as a great employer-employee relationship is one where both parties attempt to ensure the success of the other.

From an accounting perspective, this can be a very confusing concept and result in extremely messy books and records. Net checks, as outlined in the example above, are the net after tax and deductions that an employee receives for a given payroll cycle.

Net checks are similar to the ACH for the direct deposits: This money is owed to the employee. The checks should be entered into QuickBooks and dated the date of the payroll journal entry. This ensures, first, that the proper money due to the employees has been allocated to them, and, two, that all employee-related expenses are properly accrued in the correct period.

DATING THE PAYROLL JOURNAL ENTRY

Under accrual-based accounting, the payroll services rendered should be expensed in the period the work was performed, so this expense can be attributed to the sales during that period. This means the payroll journal entry should be dated the last day of the pay period to which the payment for wages correspond. In practical terms, if the pay period ends on Friday August 2, 2019, the journal entry should be dated Friday August 2, 2019. Though the funds may not be withdrawn until later, dating the journal entry in the period corresponding to the services provided ensures that you have an accurate representation of the profit and loss for the period and are following the accrual accounting methodology.

PAYROLL ACCRUAL

As a normal component of the monthly close process (an accounting procedure I recommend and explain in Chapter 12), generating a payroll accrual ensures that the books reflect the reality of the period's financial performance.

In layman's terms, by entering a payroll accrual, you ensure that expenses are not understated (for example, missing days of payroll) or overstated (for example, including too many days of payroll).

The concept is a bit confusing at first touch, but let's take a crack at it together. For most small- to midsize restaurants, a normal pay period has seven days. Most months vary in number of days. This means schedules rarely align. Therefore, if a payroll journal is entered every Friday (because in this example, Friday is the last day of the pay period), then one month may have more or fewer Fridays than another month, resulting in larger or smaller payroll expense relative to other months.

As you start to catch on, you see that the goal is not to simply move the payroll entries around but to ensure that month 1 and month 2 both include their respective payroll expense for the period.

Let's take a look at an example of payroll accrual from a restaurant that operates a fiscal year on a 12-month period, that accrues payroll over a 7-day pay period, and for which the end of the pay period is on a Friday.

For this restaurant, let's assume that February ends on Thursday, so March 1 is a Friday. Logically, the journal entry for the payroll for the period ending in February is entered on the last day of the period, March 1. Now, as you know, I have now allocated that entire week's wages into March, while in fact only one of the seven days of wages were actually expenses in the March period.

Therefore, to allocate February wages to February and March wages to March, you use a simple calculation, explained below.

Conceptually, you simply attempt to match revenue with its related expenses, and a simple accrual helps with this. This means that instead of showing abnormally high wages in March and reduced wages in February, you can understand your profitability for each period in its true form when you run the profit and loss statement in QuickBooks or prepare the monthly financial reports.

PAYROLL ACCRUAL EXAMPLE

Every month to close the books and records, you must create a payroll accrual to close the month. Below, I walk through a simple example so you understand the payroll accrual logic. Once you capture the logic, I will show you how to use QuickBooks to make the payroll accrual journal entry.

Let's take a look at a new example in which we assume the total payroll expense for the period was $7,000. Based on our example above, I have a 7-day pay period split over two months. One day is represented in March while the other six are represented in February.

SUNDAY	MONDAY	TUESDAY	WEDNESDAY	THURSDAY	FRIDAY	SATURDAY
27	28	29	30	31	1	2
3	4	5	6	7	8	9
10	11	12	13	14	15	16
17	18	19	20	21	22	23
24	25	26	27	28	1	2

To put it another way, 1 of 7 of the week's wages belong in March, while 6 of 7 of the week's wages belong in February.

Let's simply convert these wages from a percentage to a whole dollar amount to use for our accrual.

$7,000 x 1/7 = $1,000

$7,000 x 6/7 = $6,000

Always double check yourself to ensure that the entry will balance.

$1,000 + $6,000 = $7,000

Yes, it balances!

Now, since you are accruing the wage expense in February, you will use the following journal entry and its associated reversal to generate the accrual.

Date: 02/28/2019		
ACCOUNT NAME	DEBIT	CREDIT
6011 - FOH Wages: FOH Management	$6,000	
2230 - Accrued Expenses		$6,000
Total	$6,000	$6,000

Because you are reversing this in the March period, you need to enter the below entry in March. This ensures that the accrued expense balance sheet item is balanced as well as your payroll expense for the year.

Date: 03/01/2019		
ACCOUNT NAME	DEBIT	CREDIT
6011 - FOH Wages: FOH Management		$6,000
2230 - Accrued Expenses	$6,000	
Total	$6,000	$6,000

The above example uses only one department to display a payroll accrual. Remember, you should accrue all wages for your restaurant, both management and hourly. The actual accrual will be a bit more complex than the above items.

CONCLUSION

Both the payroll journal entry and monthly accrual may seem daunting at first. Don't let that hinder you from using this method. In fact, restaurant payroll accounting done right can help drive the business forward by leaps and bounds. Payroll will be one of the largest costs to your restaurant over the long-term. Knowing the true cost of payroll for the period broken out by the main cost drivers helps the management and ownership team make better decisions. Isn't it time you made better decisions?

While it may seem that the payroll journal entry can become complex, having inaccurate financials because you just cleared the payroll process withdrawals and net checks greatly outweighs the challenges. Along with this chapter and a great restaurant accounting advisor, you can have the knowledge and confidence to prepare accurate and timely financials.

BASICS OF BANKING

DAY-TO-DAY BANKING

One of the core functions of any accounting software, QuickBooks included, is to track the transactions that occur within your business. Many years ago, these transactions had to be manually tracked. That's right, entered by hand, tallied by hand, and verified by hand.

Hopefully, you no longer perform your daily transaction entry by hand, but if you do, that's okay because this chapter will help you avoid this going forward.

The key to banking with accounting software in today's business world is to leverage automation. QuickBooks software automates a majority of the transactions that make up your general ledger. The less time you spend handling your accounting, the more time you have to spend on other things, like running your business, handling HR, or greeting guests.

DAY-TO-DAY BANKING FOR RESTAURANTS

Why is day-to-day banking so crucial for restaurants? Your restaurant, like most restaurants, operates on slim margins. This means cash is not always plentiful. By knowing the exact amounts of both cash on hand and cash in the bank account, you can ensure constant liquidity. This means you can ensure that your bills are paid on time and that your vendors keep delivering. The key to business is surviving the lean times, and properly having your banking and correlated balance accurate and up-to-date is a main component of this.

THE IMPORTANCE OF THE RIGHT SET-UP

Proper banking depends on setting it up correctly from the get-go. This means setting up QuickBooks to download the right transactions into the right accounts, ensuring all transactions automatically appear inside the QuickBooks program, or perhaps going as far as having these transactions auto-sorted with built-in QuickBooks tools.

Why does proper set-up matter? Well by configuring QuickBooks correctly right from the start, your reconciliations—and subsequently your month close—will be a breeze. Basically, QuickBooks will ensure that the transactions that will likely appear on your bank statement are automatically downloaded so you can match and sort them.

You don't need me to tell you that entering all your transactions by receipts or bill payments is not only tedious, it also often results in a headache when you reconcile your books because transactions are almost always missed!

SETTING UP ACCOUNTS

In this section, I will cover bank feeds. Bank feeds are the feature in QuickBooks that lets you connect your account software directly to your financial institution (bank provider, credit card provider, and so forth). Once you have connected to this provider, the data can be pulled down automatically from the financial institution and added to QuickBooks. This is a convenient, time-saving feature that eliminates a significant amount of data entry. Remember, each bank account has a separate feed, and you need to map or connect all of them.

QUICKBOOKS DESKTOP

Before beginning, I recommend using the import web connect file option. This is the concept of downloading all the transactions from the bank and uploading them to QuickBooks. This ensures you have limited fees, no duplication, and limited issues.

1) Visit your financial institution on your web login. Select the period you would like to import your bank history from; then, download in QuickBooks Web Connect (QBO).

2) Log in to QuickBooks Desktop.

3) Visit the banking navigation at the top of the page. Then select Bank Feeds from the drop-down.

4) Next, select Import Web Connect File.

5) Select the file you downloaded from your financial institution in step 1.

6) Ensure that the Success screen appears; then proceed to step 7. If notified of error, diagnose the error.

7) The first time you import the bank feed, you will be prompted to either map your bank feed to a current bank account or create a new chart of accounts for your bank feed.

8) Once your import is complete, visit Banking, then Bank Feeds, and finally the Bank Feeds Center.

9) Select the account for which you would like to review the bank feeds.

10) If transactions are available for coding, which allows you to indicate to which chart of accounts the transaction should be mapped, the transaction list button will appear indicating the number of transactions to be coded. Simply select the Transaction List button.

QUICKBOOKS ONLINE

1) Before setting up your bank feeds, I recommend you review the information about chart of accounts in Chapter 4. Either visit your chart of accounts and add the bank accounts you will be adding or choose to add those bank accounts when you add an account below (QuickBooks Online will prompt you to add these accounts).

2) Log in to your QuickBooks Online account.

3) From the dashboard overview page, find the banking option on the left side of the screen (currently directly below the dashboard option).

4) After selecting the banking option, locate and select the green button in the top right titled Add Account.

5) This will bring you to a screen where you can select your financial institution; if you do not see your institution displayed, search your bank name or url.

6) Next, simply sign into your bank account. For those of you with multiple accounts, you can choose to give access to QuickBooks Online for some or all of these accounts.

7) Once you have granted access to your financial institution, you can match the accounts you have granted access to with the accounts in your chart of accounts. If you do not have these accounts created in your chart of accounts, simply follow the prompts to create new accounts.

8) Connect all these accounts and wait for your bank feed to download to QuickBooks Online. Note, for new accounts or accounts with lots of transactions, this may be a time-consuming process.

Do you have multiple financial institutions? Simply rinse and repeat for the previous steps. Yes, credit cards work with bank feeds as well, just remember to set them up as credit cards!

RECOMMENDED CONFIGURATION FOR RESTAURANTS

Oftentimes, when I start working with a restaurant, they may have one bank account or many bank accounts, but they typically use just one bank account for everything.

Yes, yes, using just one account is the simplest way to go about managing all the money that flows in and out. But, as you have probably already learned, the easiest way is usually not the right way, nor is it the way your business will thrive for the long-term. Simply flowing everything through one account can result in money that was allocated for sales tax being spent on payroll, money allocated for uncleared payroll checks allocated for vendor payments, and so on. While it may be easiest to keep all the money in one account, this usually results in a situation in which money allocated for one part of the business is borrowed for another, creating a vicious negative cycle.

So what configuration do I recommend for small businesses? A simple, three-account solution: one checking account for operating, one checking account for payroll, and one savings account for sales tax. I will dive into why this configuration is the correct and best setup for your small- to midsize restaurant.

These three accounts might seem overwhelming at first. However, there is a rhyme and reason for using them. Let's dive into a few good reasons for maintaining a three-account configuration:

1) Fraud occurs every day.

Small businesses with under 100 employees are more likely targets of fraud than their large counterparts. What does this mean? It means that your restaurant probably does not have all the controls in place to avoid fraud, nor the time and capital to combat it. Using this multi-account trick ensures you take a proactive approach to fraud.

2) Payroll cannot be paid late.

Payroll is one of the only expenses that cannot be paid late. Everything from rent to credit cards to vendors can be paid late (though I would advise against it). However, if employees are paid late, the Department of Labor gets involved. And by the time it gets involved, your employees have likely already quit, so it's a moot point.

3) Sales tax fines and fees have serious consequences.

What happens when you pay sales tax late or underpay? There are huge ramifications, including lots of fines and fees that quickly add up and compound. These vary from region to region. The overall point that you should make note of is that your sales tax is due and you should pay in full, even if something else needs to be missed.

4) Sales tax is not your money to spend.

A concept lots of small business owners struggle with is the concept that sales tax money is not their money. The money is the government's money and is held in trust for the government. That's right, the money is not yours, you should not spend it to pay your vendors for the most recent meat order. It's that simple, so keep the money in a separate account and don't spend it!

5) Cash flow management for small business is hard.

What's harder than starting a small business? Managing the cash flow for a small business (as I'm sure you are already well aware). When the bills are due at the end of a slow month, who should you pay? Which vendor gets a check and which vendor does not? This is one of the most challenging parts of a small business, and the three-account system will ensure you pay the most important bills first—payroll and sales tax.

PROCESSING THE BANK FEED

As mentioned earlier, QuickBooks has a time-saving feature known as the Bank Feed, which includes transactions from your bank. These transactions are usually auto sorted by QuickBooks, but this sorting isn't always accurate. That is why it's important to regularly review these transactions and classify them to your chart of accounts.

On a regular basis, these transactions need to be pulled down from your financial institution and classified to the correct chart of accounts. QuickBooks attempts to remember entries from the past and applies those changes to current transactions. For example, do you fuel up the work truck at Exxon Fuel on a regular basis? Well, QuickBooks Online remembers the classification for Exxon and attempts to auto-sort this transaction the next time you purchase from there.

Unfortunately, this is not a failsafe. Meaning that like most technology, it is great until it isn't. Don't expect QuickBooks to remember all your transactions, and it sometimes sorts them wrong or incorrectly. Review all these transactions and match them before simply approving. To do this, follow the procedure below:

UPDATING THE BANK FEED IN QUICKBOOKS DESKTOP

1) Go to the Banking button in the top navigation bar, select Bank Feeds and the choose Bank Feeds Center.
2) Once there, select the account you would like to work on (they are located under Bank Accounts on the left side of the new pop up).
3) The selection you make will be slightly greyed.
4) From that window, select the Transaction List button located on the right part of the Bank Feeds window.
5) A colored bar will appear letting you know which items

need your review (these are colored orange), which items were automatically changed by rules (these are colored red), and which were automatically matched (these are colored blue).

6) Enter the payee and related account in the current screen.

7) Choose the action button on the left side to Quick Add, Add More Details, Match to Existing Transaction, or Ignore.

8) If you prefer to perform batch transactions, you can select the check box to the left of the transactions and select batch actions from the bottom of the screen. There you can batch Add/Approve or Ignore.

UPDATING THE BANK FEED IN QUICKBOOKS ONLINE

Updating means bringing new transactions that have been processed by your financial institution into QuickBooks Online. This tends to happen automatically at night, but sometimes requires a manual update as outlined below:

1) Log in to QuickBooks Online.

2) Visit the Banking Center, located under the dashboard on the left main navigation.

3) Ensure you have connected your bank feeds per the previous section.

4) Select the Update button located near the top right of the screen (under the gear and the plus button).

5) The transactions should appear under their respective accounts. Remember, these are only the transactions that have cleared the bank or credit account.

PROCESSING THE BANK FEED IN QUICKBOOKS ONLINE

After updating the bank feed, you will need to process it. Processing is the concept of sorting transactions to the chart of accounts and creating the general ledger. Bank and credit card accounts are located in the banking portion of QuickBooks Online. The different accounts appear as cards along the top of the page. After updating your bank feeds, you can select a card in order to work with the transactions in that account.

1) By default, transactions are listed numerically. The most recent transactions appear first and are followed by the older transactions. The bank feed center can be sorted by your preference.

2) The transactions are broken up into three parts: For Review, In QuickBooks, and Excluded. Your main focus will be the For Review section—unless you need to undo a mistake (this can be done in the In QuickBooks section), you will not need to use the other categories.

3) Start with the most dated transactions and work forward.

4) Next, take a specific action for each transaction. QuickBooks shows you a suggested action to take, usually add or match (and sometimes transfer). Take the correct action for your specific transaction.

5) To clear transactions, you will choose to match or add. Remember! Some transactions will recommend you match to an incorrect transaction, so make sure you apply the right transaction to the right match.

6) If the transaction does not have a match and you choose to add it, ensure that you have found the payee from the drop-down or add the payee. A payee is either a vendor or a customer, depending on if the transaction is a cash inflow or an outflow.

PRO TIP

Sometimes you may want to split a transaction between multiple categories. To do so, simply select the transaction in question. Then select the Split button. For example did you run out to the grocery store to pick up some juice and vegetables that you were running out of? Those appear as one transaction in your bank account but need to be split between N/A Beverage and Grocery cost.

SETTING BANK FEED RULES TO MINIMIZE WORKLOAD

Bank feeds provide a pivotal way to optimize your QuickBooks work-flow. By setting up rules to automatically sort transactions you see on a regular basis, you can automatically sort these and review in seconds. For a small- to midsize restaurant, this can save hours on a weekly basis.

QUICKBOOKS DESKTOP

1) From the home screen, select Banking from the top navigation.
2) Then choose Bank Feeds from the drop-down and choose Bank Feeds Center from the additional drop-down.
3) From the top of the Bank Feeds screen, select Rules.
4) On the bottom left, select Manage Rules and choose Add New from the option menu.
5) Enter a name for the rule.
6) Select criteria to match to a transaction—either contains, starts with, ends with, matches exactly, or does not contain. (Multiple options can be chosen if preferred.)

7) Then choose how to sort the transaction per your bank rules by naming a payee and chart of accounts item.

8) Choose save to save and close this bank rule.

QUICKBOOKS ONLINE

1) From the main menu located on the left side of the screen select Banking.

2) Then from the middle navigation select Rules.

3) Select the New Rule option from the top right.

4) Enter a name for the rule.

5) From the For drop-down, select Money In or Money Out.

6) From the In drop-down, select one of your banking or credit card accounts.

7) Set the rule conditions, specifying if the transaction must meet all or any of the conditions outlined below.

8) Select the settings for the rule: Enter the transaction type, payee, and the category to apply to this transaction.

9) When complete, select save at the bottom right of the screen.

ADDING A MISSED TRANSACTION TO THE LEDGER

Often transactions are missed. Perhaps the download did not come through or the transaction was accidentally deleted. Or perhaps a transaction was matched to a duplicate transaction.

That's all okay because the transactions can simply be added back to the general ledger via the chart of accounts ledger. This is much easier than it sounds. Let's take a look.

QUICKBOOKS DESKTOP

Access the ledger in which you would like to include an additional transaction.

1) From the home screen select Check Register on the right side of the screen (or select Company from the top navigation).

2) If accessing the ledger from the top navigation, select Chart of Accounts from the drop-down, then select the ledger you would like to access.

3) If accessing after selecting Check Register, simply choose the ledger account that you would like to access.

Enter a transaction into the ledger.

1) From the Ledger screen, select the date of the transaction you would like to add on the left side of the screen.

2) Enter the transaction number (only necessary if it is a check), enter the payee, amount of payment of deposit, chart of account, and a memo to reference in the future.

3) Then select Record at the bottom right.

QUICKBOOKS ONLINE

Access the ledger in which you would like to include an additional transaction.

1) From the home screen, select Accounting on the main navigation bar located on the left side of the screen.

2) Select View Register on the left side of the screen.

Enter a transaction into the ledger.

1) From the ledger screen, select the Add Expense button from the middle left of the screen.

2) If you would like to add an expense, proceed as is; if not, select the down triangle to perform a different action.

3) Select the appropriate date of the transaction, enter a reference number (only necessary with checks), payee, memo payment, and the chart of account for the entry.

4) Choose save from the bottom right to complete the transaction.

CONCLUSION

Historically, one of the most time-consuming aspects of accounting was recording every individual transaction. Now with the advent of technology and automation, transactions no longer have to be entered manually. This entire chapter helps you optimize this workflow. Why? Because you can save hours every week by setting up proper automated transaction downloads and classification rules. Get your time back by leveraging the tools that QuickBooks Desktop and QuickBooks Online have built into their software. Say goodbye to manual entries!

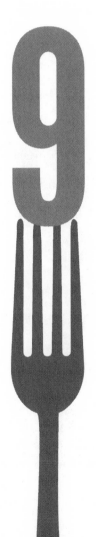

9

PAYABLES

NET, TOMORROW

Some days it feels like you owe everyone, from the beer distributor, to employees to your preferred meat vendor. This inundation of I-owe-yous can burn a business owner out in a blink of an eye. This chapter is dedicated to creating a proper accounts payable cycle to help you manage these challenges and stresses and to help you pinpoint pain points prior to them turning into real issues (like late payments). Knowing who you owe and what you owe them, and ensuring you are able to track it all in a simple report will not only alleviate stress, it will also make you a better business owner.

PAYABLES, WHAT?

One of the principal pieces of proper restaurant accounting and bookkeeping is often overlooked. Yes, proper financial reporting, tax prep, and all those items are important. But more important than all of that is knowing who you owe and how much you owe them, and then ensuring that those vendors and partners get paid.

Without proper payables management, your business will fail. When vendors don't get paid, they no longer deliver, and you as the business operator no longer have the necessary component pieces to run your restaurant.

As I stated in Chapter 3, accounts payable are as follows:

ACCOUNTS PAYABLE

Accounts payable (A/P) is the amount a business owes its suppliers or creditors. Oftentimes these are debts that must be paid off within a given period to avoid default. On many companies' balance sheets, accounts payable is often logged as a current liability.

The payable is essentially a short-term IOU from the business to the other business, which acts as a creditor.

 Restaurant Industry Context: Accounts payable is created when you enter a bill from your food, liquor, or beer supplier. This amount increases when you add a bill and decreases when you pay a bill.

PAYABLES ARE IMPORTANT

The lifeblood to any small business is readily accessible cash. This can be used to cover payroll or to pay bills. However the funds are used, properly managing this cash outflow and the related purchases will define the fate of the restaurant over the long-term.

SETTING UP VENDORS

Both QuickBooks Online and QuickBooks Desktop have an area of the software known conceptually as the Vendor Center. Though QuickBooks Online has a trendier name for this area of the application, calling it Expenses, they both serve the same basic functions. This area of the software focuses on vendor payments and organizing expenses. Below are instructions for setting up a vendor in both applications:

QUICKBOOKS DESKTOP

1) Log in to QuickBooks Desktop.
2) Visit the top navigation bar and select Vendors.
3) From the drop-down, select Vendor Center.
4) Under the subnavigation bar, select New Vendor from the top left.
5) Then, fill in as much information as you can, such as company name, address, email address, and more.

QUICKBOOKS ONLINE
1) Log in to QuickBooks Online.
2) Visit the left navigation bar and select Expenses.
3) Under the subnavigation bar, select Vendor from the top left (this will be the second choice in).
4) Select New Vendor from the top right.
5) Then, fill in as much information as you can, such as company name, address, email address, and more.

- -

PRO TIP

Entering your vendor information correctly will allow you to seamlessly pay vendors and print their checks. The net result for a small restaurant can be 30 minutes to an hour of saved time from not having to handwrite checks and hand enter information into QuickBooks.

- -

ACCOUNTS PAYABLE CYCLE
The key to keeping accrual-based accounting records is the accounts payable cycle. This helps you to track invoices based on the dates services are rendered and track payments as they flow out. Here is the detailed version:

1) Enter bills into the Vendor Center.
2) Track bills through the unpaid bill report.
3) Pay bills through the Vendor Center.
4) Print checks through QuickBooks.

The process sounds simple—and it is—but it ensures that invoices are entered properly and that they are verified for accuracy numerous times (both on bill entry and on verification when checks are printed). Additionally, accrual-based accounting and the proper accounts payable cycle sets the restaurant up to properly manage cash flow from the start.

ENTER BILLS

Managing accounts payable is often an overlooked aspect of managing a company's accounting. Done correctly, it can create significant working capital for the business, drive costs down, and more. By paying bills based on net terms, not early and not late, you help put additional cash into the business coffers. Properly reviewing and confirming the accuracy of every invoice can ensure no vendor is accidentally overpaid. So, let's walk through the process of entering bills:

1) Ask the department head responsible for the vendor relationship to review the invoice prior to submission.
2) Review the invoice again for accuracy.
3) Follow up with the vendor about any necessary credits or issues.
4) Open the Enter Bills function in QuickBooks.
5) Enter all necessary items based on the chart of accounts provided in this book.
6) Ensure the invoice date, net terms, and due date are all correct.

ENTERING BILLS IN QUICKBOOKS DESKTOP

1) On the home screen you can select Enter Bills or visit the

Vendor drop-down from the main navigation, there you can select Enter Bills.

2) Simply enter all invoice-related items, such as date, reference number (usually the invoice number), amount due, terms, due date, and all related accounts and their figures.

ENTERING BILLS IN QUICKBOOKS ONLINE

1) From the dashboard select the plus icon from the top right of the screen.

2) There, under Vendors in the drop-down, select Bill.

3) Simply enter all invoice related items, such as date, reference number (usually the invoice number), amount due, terms, due date, and all related accounts and their figures.

VENDOR CREDITS

Vendor credits have a similar entry process as bills, but credits, as you know, are the opposite of a bill and mean that a vendor owes you money.

ENTERING VENDOR CREDITS IN QUICKBOOKS DESKTOP

1) From the home screen, select Enter Bills & Vendor Credits.

2) Or from the top navigation bar under the Vendors option, select the Enter Bills option from the drop-down.

3) On the middle left of the screen, above Bill, select the option for Credit.

4) It should now say Credit.

5) Enter all credit related information and select save and close from the bottom right.

ENTERING VENDOR CREDITS IN QUICKBOOKS ONLINE
1) From the home screen, select the plus button from the top right on the screen.
2) There under Vendors, select Vendor Credit.
3) Enter all credit related information, then select save and close.

UNPAID BILLS REPORT

Tracking who you owe, how much you owe, and when you owe them is crucial to managing cash flow. The makers of QuickBooks know its importance, so have a specific report for it. This is the unpaid bills report. It shows all payables due and allows you to customize the report as you see fit.

I recommend using this report weekly, whenever you pay your bills. I prefer to select the range of all available payables as this allows you to capture important bills coming due in the near future (think about a rent invoice that needs to be mailed out a few days before the first).

UNPAID BILLS REPORT QUICKBOOKS DESKTOP
1) Visit the top navigation bar from the main screen.
2) Select Reports from the drop-down.
3) Select the Vendors and Payables category.
4) Then choose the Unpaid Bills Detail report.
5) Depending on your preference, select today's date or a date in the future from the subnavigation bar.

UNPAID BILLS REPORT QUICKBOOKS ONLINE
1) Visit the Reports section on the left side of the screen.
2) There, scroll down to the What You Owe section.

3) Select the Unpaid Bills report.
4) Depending on your preference, select today's date or a date in the future from the subnavigation bar.

PAYING BILLS

If you follow the above outlined process and regularly enter your bills into QuickBooks, the accounting software will not only help you keep track of these bills but manage the process of payment as well. No, the software isn't smart enough to pay your bills for you, but it will help you seamlessly track what has been paid to ensure no duplicate payments occur.

Let's take a look at the bill payment process:

QUICKBOOKS DESKTOP

The following steps walk through the paying bills process under the premise that checks will be printed (which I highly recommend):

1) On the home screen select Pay Bills or visit the top navigation and select Vendors; from there, select the Pay Bills option from the drop-down.
2) From the Pay Bills area, you will see the invoices recently entered and not yet paid.
3) Select the bills you would like to pay via a checkmark on the left side of the screen.
4) Then verify the date is correct, and select the method as Check.
5) Then, set the option icon as To Be Printed.
6) Finally, ensure that the correct operating bank account is selected (this should match the checks you will print on).

Note: If you have manual checks, simply select Assign Check Number, and follow the same process as above.

QUICKBOOKS ONLINE

1) From the dashboard select the plus icon from the right top of the screen.
2) Then, under Vendors, select Pay Bills.
3) From the Pay Bills area, you will see the invoices recently entered and not yet paid.
4) Select the bills you would like to pay via a checkmark on the left side of the screen.
5) Ensure the correct operating bank account is selected (this should match the checks you are printing on).
6) Then select Print Later at the top of the screen, and click to save and close (bottom right).

· ·

PRO TIP

You can pay bills with a credit card, as well, and track them through the Bill Pay center.

· ·

PRINTING CHECKS

Note that printing checks should happen after Bill Pay for all items that are not paid via credit card, ACH, or wire transfer.

QUICKBOOKS DESKTOP

1) From the home screen, select the Print Checks option, located on the bottom right of the screen.

2) Or select banking from the top navigation bar and choose Write Checks. From that window, select the small down arrow under Print and then choose Batch.

3) Select the bank account you set the bill payments to print from.

4) Choose the check or checks via checkmarks on the left side of the screen (you can also simply Select All, if preferred).

5) Match your physical starting check with the First Check Number.

6) Click OK and follow the onscreen prompts.

QUICKBOOKS ONLINE

1) From the home screen, select the plus icon at the top right of the screen.

2) Then under Vendors, choose the Print Checks option.

3) Select the bank account you have set the previous bill payments to print from.

4) Choose the check or checks via checkmarks from the left side of the screen (simply click the top checkmark located by date to select all).

5) Then select Preview and Print from the bottom right and follow the onscreen prompts.

APPLYING VENDOR CREDITS

QUICKBOOKS DESKTOP

1) When in the process of paying bills (refer to the how-to above), select the bill payment you would like to apply the credit to.

2) This can be done by ensuring the bill is selected via the checkmark on the left side of the screen.

3) Then, select the bill to apply the credit; ensure it is

highlighted, and then choose Set Credits near the bottom middle of the screen.

4) A new screen will pop up listing all the credits available to apply.

5) To apply any of the available credits, simply use the check mark on the left side of the screen and click Done.

6) If done properly, the Credits Used column will display the previously selected dollar amounts and the Amount to Pay will be net those credits.

QUICKBOOKS ONLINE

1) When in the process of paying bills (refer to the how-to above), and when selecting a vendor with an open vendor credit, the vendor credit will auto populate.

This is a great feature that helps make the bill paying process a bit quicker, though for those who prefer to select their own credits to apply, there is another process.

1) From the home screen, select the Expense option on the left navigation bar.

2) Choose the Vendor from the middle horizontal navigation.

3) Select the vendor via search or by scrolling down.

4) Once the vendor has been selected, choose which bill you would like to make payment on.

5) Simply select Make Payment from the right side of the screen adjacent to the bill needing to be paid.

6) Scrolling down from this screen, you can select which credits to utilize against this bill payment.

7) If you would like this check included in your normal check run, simply select to print later.

MISCELLANEOUS CHECKS

Restaurant owners regularly need to send out miscellaneous or random checks that are not associated with the regular bill payment cycle. Below I walk you through processing this kind of check.

QUICKBOOKS DESKTOP

1) From the home screen, select Write Checks from the bottom right of the screen.
2) Or from the top navigation, select Banking and then Write Checks from the drop-down.
3) Select the bank account you'll use for the check (it should match the account information on your check).
4) Complete the vendor, check number, date, amount, and account codes for this transaction.
5) If you need to print this check (meaning, it is not handwritten or already sent out), select the print option from the top middle of the screen.

QUICKBOOKS ONLINE

1) From the home screen, click on the plus icon at the top right of the screen.
2) Underneath Vendors, select Check.
3) Complete the vendor, check number (or set to print), category, description, and amount.
4) If this is a handwritten check, simply fill in the check number.
5) Then select save and close.

CONCLUSION

This chapter aims to acquaint you with the best practices for accounts payable and to give you straightforward steps for performing these functions within the QuickBooks realm. Payables are one of the main accounting functions and managing this process effectively will ensure your restaurant's long-term success. Remember, many great restaurants have gone out of business because they did not pay their bills.

10 RESTAURANT INVENTORY

INVENTORY

Inventory is the fundamental component of most (nonsoftware related) businesses. It is often the bane of most small business owners' existence, however, because there is never enough of it, and all excess capital always seems to end up there. Yet inventory is also the biggest overlooked opportunity as well, because properly optimizing inventory management can help generate significant working capital inside the business.

RESTAURANT INVENTORY

Did you know that restaurants have one of the most challenging inventories to manage? Not simply because of the sheer number of different components that each dish or beverage requires, but because inventory can spoil before it is utilized. Most industries may be stuck with last year's style or product version, but that can at least be sold in some off-market channel or at a discounted rate. If raw chicken goes bad, it goes bad—those dollars are completely lost and unrecoverable. You probably already know this (and too well). You also probably already know that QuickBooks has a built in inventory system. What you probably didn't know is that the QuickBooks system was not designed with restaurants in mind. This chapter will show you a quicker and better system to optimize your inventory management.

ACCOUNTING FOR INVENTORY

For accounting purposes, inventory is the goods in stock at your restaurant. From a month-to-month management perspective, these items fluctuate monthly and effect your cost of goods. Before I dive too deep, though, let's look at the official definition.

Inventory is an itemized list of current assets, such as a catalog of the property of an individual or estate, or a list of goods on hand.

The key word in this definition that helps differentiate inventory from other assets in the restaurant is the phrase "current assets." These are items that can be converted to cash in less than a year. For example, if you make a sandwich and then sell that sandwich, you have converted it to cash. The bread, the mayo, the meat, and the cheese are current assets.

IMPORTANCE OF INVENTORY

It may seem easier just to avoid tracking a monthly or weekly inventory. It is extremely tedious to spend half a day counting everything!

However, while keeping track of inventory is challenging and especially when you are accounting for everything purchased within the month, it's important to understand exactly why inventory matters.

Say you sold $100,000 worth of food last month but also bought $50,000-worth of food, including meats, seafoods, frozen items, spices, and more. Just looking at those numbers and conducting a little basic math, it seems you have a 50 percent food cost. Wow, that's out of control and a bit alarming! I calculated this by taking your true food costs and dividing that by your food sales (50,000/100,000).

What this simple calculation does not account for, however, is how much of my purchases I still have on hand. Sitting in your inventory, a few things could have happened: Perhaps there was a slow week at the end of the month, which meant the restaurant carried over more product into the next week; perhaps multiple orders were received in the last few days of the month but haven't yet been used; perhaps there are significant numbers of dry or frozen goods that have not yet been consumed.

Regardless of the reason, without knowing what is in the back room or freezer, it's impossible to determine the actual amount that was consumed in order to calculate cost of goods during the period.

Let's say your inventory increased by $15,000 from the beginning of this fictitious month until the end. That means your cost of goods was reduced by $15,000 for the same period, resulting in a true cost of goods of $35,000. Our quick math has the cost of goods much nearer to 35 percent now.

This 15 percent adjustment in cost of goods means everything. This is the difference between operating a profitable restaurant or not; it's also the difference between correctly or incorrectly running a kitchen. Yes, for the pros out there, a significant increase in inventory is also always a problem, but for the sake of this basic argument, proper inventory tracking will ensure cost and inventory issues are brought to the owner's and management's attention in a timely manner to address any issues before they sink the business.

WHAT TO INVENTORY

It is very easy to start walking through your restaurant and begin counting everything. I caution you not to do this.

There are three main inventory buckets to keep track of:

1) Food Inventory
2) Beverage Inventory
3) Bar & Consumable Inventory

Before I dive deeper, stop and think about your business. Are you a coffee shop? If so, I bet your most valuable inventory is coffee. You should likely break this out to see the month to month fluctuations of this asset. Are you a steakhouse? You probably want to see what your most popular cut of meat looks like in terms of dollars on a monthly basis. Do you have a large dry stock, separate from your perishable and frozen food? Keep track of this separately. The above is a guideline: In general, keep this to three to five categories, and modify it to fit your business.

PRO TIP

Setting up inventory to match your restaurant configuration makes the monthly close process easier. For example, if you count the bar items, freezer, dry storage, and back line individually, keep track of them separately and then account for them this way within QuickBooks.

FOOD INVENTORY

These are the items related to the back of the house (also known as the kitchen, for first-time restaurateurs). This includes the freezer, walk-in, dry storage, hidden spots throughout the kitchen, the line, reach ins, and so on.

BEVERAGE INVENTORY

This would include all of your nonalcoholic beverages. Many restaurants carry unnecessary inventory without even realizing it. For example, most restaurant sit on thousands in soda syrups and do not even realize it. These are usually in box form and will be either hooked up to your soda fountain or stored somewhere ready to use.

BAR & CONSUMABLE INVENTORY

Included in this category are the beer, liquor, wine, and related alcoholic items. This would also include consumables used to make those related drinks, from the fresh fruit to the mixers. Additionally, if you use significant paper products related to your bar service, this is where you will inventory those items.

WHY INVENTORY MY WAY

Why my method? It is based on the concept of human capital. Everyone on your team, from the accounting office to the kitchen, has limited time. The most efficient way to record inventory is on a monthly basis, which means a count is required monthly. This ensures everyone's time is most efficiently utilized and the financials are correct on a monthly basis. Either way, read below and use your key takeaways to improve your process. Ensure that you have ending dollar values for your inventory so you can account for it in the next section.

QuickBooks is incredibly good at many things, but restaurant inventory is not one of them. QuickBooks's propensity to track cost of goods on a per item basis and track inventory on the balance sheet with the same per item basis means that it is not a good go-to tool for restaurant inventory tracking. This is because restaurants track and purchase inventory with multiple pack and case sizes. Additionally, the production of each plate of food or beverage varies for every item on a cost of goods production. I advise my clients—whether they're hugely successful owners of multimillion-dollar franchises or owners of intimate neighborhood coffee shops—to keep a separate record of inventory within Excel or an inventory tracking system outside QuickBooks and reconcile the books to a total dollar amount on a monthly basis.

HOW TO INVENTORY MY WAY

Excel is a powerful and useful program, a great tool for the restaurant owner and operator. By using Excel for inventory, you can quickly manage your restaurant inventory, properly update QuickBooks, and do so before the restaurant rush.

For a small restaurant owner, costing a menu is challenging enough. Now imagine if you had to calculate the cost of goods for each item sold as it went out the kitchen window for a set period. Wow! Overwhelming for sure. I can think of 10 items that are more pressing than countless hours calculating your monthly cost of goods. How about hiring that new line cook, fixing the broiler, or simply touching tables?

Restaurant inventory does not have to be an impossible task routed around trying to make impossible cost of goods accounting possible.

WHAT TO COUNT

Keeping track of exactly what items to inventory can be a bit challenging for those who do not have significant restaurant experience or are just new to the world of inventory.

A weekly or monthly inventory count does not mean you go into the kitchen and literally count everything. Most of the purchases within your kitchen or restaurant that are fixtures were either previously expensed or are treated like assets on your balance sheet, meaning, they are depreciated monthly.

When observing what to count, you want to focus on all items that are inputs into your finished product. For example, the spices used to marinate your meat, the potatoes used to make your french fries, and the hamburger meat used to make your yummy burgers. All those items are the main components in your finished product—the product that is on your menu and that you charge for.

So specifically, what do you count? When counting your food inventory, you want to focus on all perishable related items. This could be everything from tomatoes to spices to frozen goods in the freezer. All these items have value, were purchased, and should contribute to what you deem inventory on hand.

Sometimes, it is valuable to mention what not to count. Even though the broiler, propane, plates and much more go into making your restaurant run—these items do not directly contribute to what you charge the customer. For example, when a customer orders a fish plate, the fish, rice and garnish go directly into the cost of that dish. The other items mentioned a moment ago are controllable expenses related to running your restaurant, and that's why you avoid counting these.

· ·

PRO TIP

Still stuck? Feel free to send me an email at zac@zacweiner.com and we can chat through which items you should or should not be including in your regular inventory.

· ·

HOW TO SET UP YOUR INVENTORY SYSTEM

We all have a way we have done it for years. Sometimes one approach works, and sometimes it does not. Our goal here is to get an ending value for inventory at the end of each period, using the same counting, recording, and pricing technique to ensure accounting consistency.

Below is my tried and true method used with countless restaurants over the past few years.

START WITH A NOTEPAD

That's right. Take a simple blank notepad, and if you run anything other than a small café, better use legal.

Ensure production has ceased, so either early in the morning or late in the evening when you have a few hours of time to spare and no one will be in the restaurant.

Ideally, it is best to use a minimum of two individuals to perform these processes, preferably someone who knows the item case pack (how many items come into the kitchen/bar, and how they are ordered—for example, one case of tomatoes).

One person is assigned to take notes and one person is assigned to count items. Yes, communication is required to complete this task. So ensure you verbalize what you are counting.

One person verbalizes the items in front of them, counts the items, and relays that to the note taker. The note taker should record the count of each item, the type of each, and the case pack.

If it helps, sometimes I recommend recording a voice memo on your iPhone or cellular device to reference back when a note doesn't make sense. This is a definite must-do for the first three to five inventory sessions, because as you already know, taking notes but then not understanding them later negates the point of taking the notes in the first place.

ORGANIZE AND SEPARATE

Each restaurant has its own unique flow and storage configuration. Once restaurants inventory setup may not work for another. For example, one restaurant may have dry storage off the kitchen, another may have it on the second floor.

Your inventory setup, especially the first time, should be broken out by area. For example, dry storage should be counted separately, then the line, which is counted separately from the walk-in and freezer.

This accomplishes two goals: One, it makes it possible to delegate pieces of the inventory count in the future, and two, it ensures organization.

Why is organization important, you ask? Well, without organization of inventory in physical form, you will have a nearly impossible time organizing it in digital form. If one type of product is in three locations, it makes the inventory count redundant (you are counting three of the same things that all have to be recorded numerous times), and when you update your pricing sheets, you will likely be duplicating your work.

· ·

PRO TIP

If you have the same product in numerous places, it means your chef or ordering manager does not even know that he/she has duplicates. Consolidate, order fewer items, and help your cash flow.

· ·

ENTER INTO EXCEL

Once you've spent hours counting everything under the sun; organizing your products as you go; and documenting the case packs, types, and count; you have all the information necessary to set up a proper inventory system.

The information from your legal pad needs to be converted to digital form. Hello, data entry. You will set up six columns as follows:

Item

Case Pack

Price (per case pack)

Quantity

Total Value

Percentage of Total

I have already covered item, case pack, and quantity earlier in this chapter. Now, why price? Price is important in calculating the dollar value of each item. I need the dollar value of each individual item to ensure I get a dollar value for the total. The entire point of this process is to get a value of the inventory in the kitchen at one point in time, a snapshot, that is.

Total value and percentage of total are equally as important. Our total value of each item ensures that I can add this to the total value of all the other items and get a total value for an area or type of product.

Percentage of total is valuable to ensure that I know what product I have on hand. Did you know that you had a few thousand dollars in mushrooms? That accounts for 10 percent of your product. That doesn't make sense, does it? This kind of issue makes regularly reviewing inventory data valuable for managing cash flow and ensuring proper ordering.

CALCULATE TOTALS

Once you have all your information in an Excel format, you can manipulate the data. Taking a total from each area or by food type, depending on your preferred method, you can now calculate the totals.

HOW TO PERFORM A REGULAR INVENTORY

The example from above is really the framework to set up an inventory for the first time.

Once you have the Excel templates and a majority of the items regularly ordered in an accessible and consistent format, the process gets easier.

Now, the next step requires updating the Excel format to prepare for the next inventory. Change the name of column "Quantity" to "Previous Quantity."

Then, you need to update the spreadsheet to include a new column called "Current Quantity." This will be the count for your second and subsequent inventories.

Ensure that your current quantity column is empty, and modify this workbook so you can print it out. Now you have graduated from the world of legal pad to the world of printed paper. Take your printed quantities, grab your counting friend, and get counting.

Of course, there will be new items that were not included before and items that you had previously but that now have zero counts. This is especially the case if, for example, you have an ever-changing seasonal menu implementing fresh ingredients. However, even if you don't, you will likely have seasonality of purchasing throughout the year. Simply handwrite the new items and add it to the Excel document when you update your digital inventory.

Next, calculate totals, as described in the previous section. Wow! You now have an updated inventory that took half the time.

RESTAURANT INVENTORY IS DIFFERENT

Perhaps you have a few business associates in other industries. Have you ever talked about inventory? Well, if you have, you will know that their system functions very differently from yours. Let's look at an example.

George owns a t-shirt store in Laguna Beach, California. George buys shirts from a local rep and buys 100 shirts at a time. His costs are set: He paid $4 a shirt. No matter if he sells that shirt today, next week, or next year, his price is $4. His shirt does not go bad; it does not need any additional manufacturing; it does not need any additional sauce or finishing touches. Additionally, it won't be sent back to the kitchen or need to be replaced after the sale has occurred (yes, refunds do occur).

As you captured from above, restaurant inventory is different. Restaurants are one of the few businesses where inventory is literally manufactured and sold alongside a service under one roof.

This lends itself to a lot of challenges. Specifically, the cost per specific menu item sold fluctuates and is never precise. This means that conducting inventory on a per item basis as you would in a t-shirt shop is unrealistic.

Ideally, the most efficient way to manage inventory in a restaurant setting is to capture inventory at the beginning of the period, purchases during the period, and inventory at the end of the period. By using the basic inventory equation over a set period, you ensure you are not trying to calculate the impossible per item cost of goods, but rather capturing the average cost of goods over a period, such as a month. This ensures that the brunt of the work is completed on a monthly basis rather than on an—impossible—daily basis.

UPDATE INVENTORY PRICING REGULARLY

What good is an inventory count if it is not accurate? You did not spend hours counting every item in the kitchen to have an incorrect ending inventory balance.

Besides item count, pricing is the second key component to a proper inventory value. The pricing of items changes on a regular basis, sometimes due to seasonality, demand, change in vendors, rain in California, and much more.

These variables are unfortunately impossible to control. Fortunately for you, measuring their impact is controllable and will help you react to these changes quicker and with sound logic.

Updating inventory pricing can be a tedious process, but absolutely necessary. Let's take a look at how to accomplish this.

PICK A TIME PERIOD

Certain restaurants need to update their pricing more often than others. For example, a seafood restaurant that purchases local and fresh fish that regularly sees 35 percent price swings needs to update its pricing more often than say a large corporate franchise that sets pricing well into the future.

If your product experiences regular price swings, you should update your pricing on a regular basis. This means if you inventory weekly, you should update pricing biweekly. If you update inventory biweekly, you should update pricing bimonthly.

Those that have more normalized pricing, without large pricing swings in high-dollar items, can update on a less frequent basis. If you inventory weekly, or biweekly, updated pricing monthly is sufficient. For those that inventory monthly, updating pricing quarterly is enough.

PRO TIP

Pick a system and stick to it. Choose a methodology for updating pricing and use this consistently all year round.

ENTERING A JOURNAL ENTRY IN QUICKBOOKS

To properly record inventory in the method I outline, you need to be able to create a journal entry in QuickBooks. I covered this earlier in the book in Chapter 5 but a refresher is always valuable.

Remember, a journal entry is a basic accounting transaction. A basic rule of journal entries is that the total of the debit column must equal the total of the credits column.

As shown below, journal entries are useful when recording transfers from an asset, liability, or equity account to an income or expense account or vice versa.

QUICKBOOKS DESKTOP

1) Select the Company button in the home navigation bar at the top of the QuickBooks Desktop screen.
2) From the drop-down, select Make General Journal Entries.
3) Some users may see a notification letting them know that QuickBooks automatically numbers journal entries. You can eventually turn off auto-sequencing or change the beginning number, but for now, just click OK to enter your journal entry.
4) Once the journal entry screen populates, select the appropriate date (from the drop-down), title the journal entry, enter the date, credit account name, debit account name, credit amounts, and debit amounts.

QUICKBOOKS ONLINE

1) Select the plus icon located at the top right of the QuickBooks Online screen.
2) Then select Journal Entry from the drop-down.
3) Once the journal entry screen populates, select the appropriate date and enter the relevant journal entry name.
4) Yes, it's that easy!

In the coming sections, you'll find the appropriate information to enter the correct name, date, credit accounts, debit accounts, credit amounts, and debit amounts. I will also highlight account names and associated dollar amounts to use.

RECORDING INVENTORY INSIDE QUICKBOOKS

Since this book is about QuickBooks, it is very important that I show how this is accomplished. However, unlike other books on this topic, I do not just want you to enter what you assume is your inventory value, I want you to go through the above-mentioned steps so that you have an accurate and updated inventory. If you do this, the financials you review will be just that—accurate and up-to-date.

As mentioned earlier, the built-in inventory systems within QuickBooks are both challenging and complex for the first-time user. Additionally, they were designed without restaurants in mind. So, instead of using this system, you will create a journal entry on a monthly basis to record your change in inventory.

I will walk through two different scenarios that you will encounter: an increase in inventory and a decrease in inventory. During any one period, you may have beverage inventory that increases and food inventory that decreases or vice versa. This is quite normal.

INCREASE IN INVENTORY

This example shows you what happens when your inventory increases from the previous month. For example, say you're finishing July reporting, and your food inventory is valued at $1,500. Last month at the end of June, your food inventory was valued at $1,250, and you recorded this in your books.

Now, let's create a journal entry:

I will use two items from your chart of accounts: Change in Food Inventory (Cost of Goods) and Food Inventory (Asset).

	DEBIT	CREDIT
5190 - Change in Food Inventory	$250	
1210 - Food Inventory		$250

DECREASE IN INVENTORY

Let's reverse the example so you can see the opposite case. This example shows you what happens when your inventory decreases from the previous month. For example, say you're finishing July reporting, and your food inventory is valued at $1,500. Last month at the end of June, your food inventory was valued at $1,750, and you recorded this in your books.

I will be using two items from your chart of accounts: Change in Food Inventory (Cost of Goods) and Food Inventory (Asset).

	DEBIT	CREDIT
5190 - Change in Food Inventory		$250
1210 - Food Inventory	$250	

ELATION (AND CONCLUSION)

Hopefully the simplified method referenced in this chapter caused you to feel some form of elation. Though some steps are still there and still challenging—like the manual inventory count—the fact of the matter is we have removed the burdensome QuickBooks piece that was simply not designed with restaurants in mind. This chapter set out to give you the most cost-effective system for inventory success, so implement it into your day-to-day restaurant management.

11

SET A WEEKLY SCHEDULE

WHY GET ORGANIZED?

Organization for some comes with ease. For others, it's a daunting nightmare. Are you the former or the latter? If you are the former, skim the following pages. If you are the latter, read three times.

Running a restaurant is very similar to running a household. If you do not set aside the time throughout the year to clean or do not bring in a maid to clean, your home will be disgusting by the end of the year. If you do not have a family calendar on the fridge or on everyone's smartphone, appointments and practices will surely be missed. If you are an incredibly organized person like me, you create a schedule and set aside time every fourth weekend to do a deep cleaning and every other weekend do a light cleaning. If you are like me, you have a calendar shared on your smartphone and an itemized shopping list shared in a to-do application. It is very likely that you are not like me yet, and that is why I will give you the tools you need to get organized.

In the world of accounting, lack of structure means lack of organization, which results in missing important dates and deadlines, often with very serious ramifications. What would your employees do if you missed their direct deposit deadline week after week? They would go work for someone else! What would your vendors do if they were paid late week after week? They would surely stop delivering to you. No matter how understanding and caring a leader you are, if you don't stay organized, you are burning your organization down from the inside.

RESTAURANT ORGANIZATION

Often, as you get a restaurant off the ground, or as you inherit systems from previous owners and managers, things are done a certain way just because. This is not a good reason to do things. Having been in similar shoes, I've written this chapter to explain the major accounting elements you need for optimum weekly maintenance. It's a simple guide to get you going in the right direction, but its goal is to help you use the material to best fit your lifestyle.

WHY WEEKLY?

Choosing a weekly structure is not a lucky guess or some crazy idea pulled from the sky. To make conscious and accurate business decisions, you need data on a regular and routine basis. A weekly schedule is neither too short not too long. Accounting on a weekly basis allows you to look at the minor details of your organization and catch oddities before they become nuclear disasters.

All restaurants live and breathe by cash flow, and employees are often paid on a weekly basis to properly manage this cash flow. By looking at sales over cost of goods sold and expenses (such as payroll), you can quickly map a structure through which to learn in-depth about your business.

A weekly structure also makes sense for a less profound reason— we typically think in days. We plan our weeks around which night we will cook in or go out to eat. We plan our weeks around which days the kids are going to what practice. We plan our life around weeks. As a restaurant owner, you plan your week according to which nights you will be at your restaurant.

In terms of business, a weekly structure just makes sense. Although some owners may do cash deposits on the third Tuesday of the month, this isn't a good idea. Why wait to put cash into the bank for almost 30 days? Don't you need that cash to pay weekly bills?

Waiting every four weeks to deposit cash is asking for a disaster situation and an inability to pay the bills.

Now, when I say you need to deposit cash weekly, the wheels in your head might start turning. You may say to yourself, well, my daughter's softball practice is Thursday evening at 6—the bank is on the way, why not stop then? Now instead of creating a complex schedule that makes your life more challenging, you've integrated your new task into your current schedule.

Perhaps you do not have kids, but you always have lunch in the same shopping area on Saturday. I guarantee that you will find one bank open on Saturday, or your bank will allow for an overnight deposit. Either way, you can deposit the cash on the way to your favorite lunch spot without worrying about compromising your life or not accomplishing the task on a weekly basis.

RESTAURANTS PLAN IN WEEKS

Often, planning in weeks comes up in conversation with my small business-owning clients. Weekly planning is by far the most important for the restaurant owners I work with. This is due to a few reasons:

1) Employees are scheduled weekly.

Every week a schedule comes out, this is fairly normal across all restaurants. Sometimes two weeks are published at once, but most of the time employees are scheduled weekly and everyone in the restaurant thinks in weeks.

2) The week has its own rhythm.

That's right, just like the ebbs and flows of a month, restaurants have their ebbs and flows of the week. Monday is usually a slow day, while Thursday, Friday and Saturday are slammed. Don't forget Sunday, too, if you have a killer brunch program. So setting a schedule around when you are busier versus slower allows you to optimize your work life around when you are needed onsite. Set up your weekly rhythm to complement that of your busy restaurant life.

3) Payroll is weekly.

Restaurant employees are adamant about getting paid weekly—trust me, I have tried to change pay schedules to biweekly, and it's a battle not worth the time. Anyways, payroll is always processed on the same day; checks are always ready in the office on the same day. If this routine is broken, there are 50 unhappy people calling and texting the owner or manager. The payroll routine is weekly and important for the proper flow of the restaurant.

4) Vendors deliver weekly.

For most average-sized restaurants, bespoke vendors deliver weekly. That means they usually want their check in hand before bringing the order in, especially if you are maximizing your terms (I recommend maximizing your terms). For larger operations, deliveries may be a few times a week, such as Monday, Wednesday, and Friday. Either way, these deliverers are on a set schedule. You should know this schedule, know when your checks need to be ready, and take this into account when planning your weekly schedule.

A REAL-WORLD EXAMPLE

Years ago I ran an organization with a hundred employees and a few million dollars in revenue. We did not have a complex accounting staff or much above the level of QuickBooks Pro in our toolkit, yet we were incredibly successful. What led us down the road to success, you may ask? A clear and concise weekly schedule that ensured all deposits were made and that financial information was updated, both of which helped ensure correct reporting.

Here is a version of that schedule:

MONDAY
- Check mail and invoice email inbox, record all deposits and invoices received.
- Record sales from previous week (Tuesday until Sunday).
- Update online banking (Tuesday until Friday of previous week).*

TUESDAY
- Make cash and check deposits.
- Finish online banking (for Monday).
- Finish recording sales (for Monday).
- Cut checks for the week (mailing out Tuesday will ensure receipt by Friday).

WEDNESDAY
- Review weekly profit and loss statement.
- Hold all staff meetings associated with finance.

THURSDAY
- Check mail and invoice email inbox again, record all invoices received.
- Perform weekly payroll run.

FRIDAY

- Resolve any other outstanding items (reclass expenses, follow up on payments, fix any incorrect checks, etc.).

*Saturday and Sunday banking usually do not clear until Tuesday morning.

WHY SO MANY DIFFERENT TASKS?

For owners and managers new to the accounting world, it may seem like there are a lot of different activities—as if you jump around from banking to sales to payroll. Yes, this is a bit true, but accountants and bookkeepers for small- to midsize restaurants wear a lot of hats. This is quite similar to that of owners and managers of these organizations—sometimes you have to run food to tables and wait on guests, as well.

This weekly schedule is derived with the goal of splitting all the monthly tasks up into small pieces of work that are both manageable and able to be completed within a normal work week.

At the end of the month, when your financials reporting is due and the monthly close needs to be completed, having done all these little tasks as outlined will make that process a breeze. Well, probably not a breeze at first, but much more manageable the first few times and then a cakewalk after that.

SET YOURSELF UP FOR SUCCESS

Over the years I have worked with lots of individuals and teams that waited until the last minute to accomplish all the above tasks—don't be like those people. Set yourself up for success, carve out time for your routine. Plan your days and weeks in advance.

This makes the weekly goals easier to check off the list and ensures no deadlines are missed monthly. Additionally, working for a manager or owner who has a system and plan in place increases retention. Have you ever worked for someone who was constantly running around last-minute trying to get things done and was always late to everything? It can be a major pain.

Organization and preparation make you a desirable leader. Employees work more confidently and have an increased morale when they know their check is right every week and will be in their hands at the same time every week.

WHAT'S THE LOGIC?

The above schedule is a great starter for any restaurant business. The key is not as much which days certain items are completed but rather why they were done on those days. Are you updating your banking for a meeting? Are you mailing checks out so they reach your vendor by the end of the week? Tailor the schedule to work for you and your business, just make sure you understand the logic of your choices.

The overall goal is to have accurate and true financials. What's the point of holding a weekly staff meeting and discussing your numbers if the numbers are not accurate? If you are discussing the previous week and none of the invoices are entered into the system, you are not tracking the expenses of the restaurant. If your restaurant has multiple departments (catering, BOH, FOH, bar, etc.), and you are meeting with a department head but have not reviewed the expense he or she is responsible for—what's the point of meeting? Having the tools you and your staff need to succeed are crucial to the overall success of your restaurant!

When running a small restaurant, you live and die by your numbers. These figures decide how you can grow your business, compensate yourself, and reinvest in your business (restaurant equipment always needs fixing). If your numbers are not updated on a weekly basis so you can take a look at weekly financials, then what is the point of the numbers?

Small restaurants also operate on razor thin margins, so the difference between covering payroll from one week to the next may be in whether or not you can make the weekly cash deposit. Missing a vendor invoice for a large delivery could be catastrophic, especially if they are your main vendor and you need additional items. Having everything updated, deposits made, and so on can help you properly plan your needs and allocate cash.

As a business owner, you will often have a long-term plan and a short-term plan. These plans will likely have monetary goals attached to them. By setting budget, expenses, or other operating margins against these timelines, you can see if you are succeeding or failing. Don't walk into your meetings empty handed. Ensure you follow a weekly routine, so your numbers are prepared and ready to help you make the best possible decision, because at the end of the day, it is your job as the business owner to make the best decisions for your team.

CONCLUSION

Do you ever feel like you are scrambling to catch up? Like you missed an important call, email or forgot an important to-do? It happens to the most organized of us, but when it comes to things like paying vendors and ensuring your business is cash flowing, these simply cannot be missed. Take it a step further and consider things like paying taxes, filing sales tax, and more: Missing these items have negative repercussions. In this chapter, I want to help you think through a process of creating a simple schedule for success for you and your restaurant.

12

MONTH CLOSE

THE MONTH END FOR ACCOUNTING

The month end is one of the main activities to complete in the accounting and bookkeeping role. By properly accounting for items on a monthly basis, you will make properly accounting for items on a quarterly basis that much easier. This chapter outlines all the items that need to be addressed on a monthly basis, ensuring your books are up-to-date and accurate, and the financials you prepare are truly reflective of your business.

THE MONTH END FOR RESTAURANT ACCOUNTING

As you know, the restaurant business is more complex and challenging than initially meets the eye. It is not as simple as standing behind the counter and pouring a beer (I mean where does the beer come from, and did you get credit for those old kegs!?). The restaurant month end is no different, with a lot of nuances and industry-specific ideas that make it seem daunting at first. Learning the routine and procedures as outlined below will initially feel overwhelming, but in reality, these processes will ensure all the cash and credit card monies are accounted for, financials are accurate, and you can make better business decisions about how to grow top- and bottom-line moving forward.

WHAT EXACTLY ARE YOU CLOSING—A DOOR?

Closing the month is a phrase you've definitely heard before. But what in the world does it mean? Is it the reason why accountants are always so busy the first week of the month? What in the world is going on?

Financial reporting is a valuable tool for restaurants because it helps leaders make sound decisions, and sound decisions move businesses forward. To make these strong and confident financial decisions, you must have solid financials to base decisions on.

The monthly closing process ensures that the accounting records for the previous month are accurate and representative of the business. I will go over a mini checklist, but first you must understand that if you do not have a repetitive proven process to close the books, your financials will be inaccurate.

Most of the following tasks actually occur inside QuickBooks, in both the online and desktop versions. They are tasks that ensure the information you have entered for the period is accurate and representative of the business. Some of the items are simple record keeping, like storing related statements and backup documents on a local computer or in the cloud, though these items tie hand-in-hand to the work done in QuickBooks.

TASKS TO COMPLETE AT THE END OF EACH MONTH

Below is a list of items that need to take place to properly close the month. This list is in no particular order, and you should order your list in a way that best suits your business workflow. I recommend that you do all of the following items, because picking and choosing some activities to complete and not others will result in inaccurate records, which is exactly what you do not want.

CLOSE POSTING PERIODS TO AP AND AR

After you ensure that all your payables and receivables have been recorded for the period, you should consider the period closed. That means you have entered and sent out all the invoices you are aware of for the period (this typically applies to those of you who also run a catering business). This should happen within the first week of the following month. Sometimes you will get invoices for the previous period after the period has been closed, but simply date them the date of the current month and denote in the memo the correct invoice date. Why? Because the previous period is now closed to all payables entries! If you send out financial statements and then continue to add payables and receivables, then the statements you sent out are inaccurate.

BANK RECONCILIATION

Because reconciliations are more involved than other items on the list of closing to-dos, I will treat them in Chapter 13 below. They are an important item in the closing process and are conducted after everything is entered and you have access to your bank statements.

LOAN & CREDIT CARD RECONCILIATIONS

All loan amounts on your balance sheet should tie to your most recent statements. If you owe $100,000 at the end of last month, the balance sheet should show the same amount for that date. Credit cards are also a form of loan, and credit card information should be entered and then reconciled.

PRO TIP

Credit card reconciliations can sometimes be difficult because credit card cycles do not always fall at the end of the month. The best course of action is to print your most recent transactions, from, let's say the 20th to the end of the month, and then reconcile these transactions via the Reconciliation Center of QuickBooks. Do not close the reconciliation! Just ensure all transactions are entered so your financial statement is accurate.

TIE OUT SALES TO YOUR POINT OF SALE

As was highlighted in this book, your POS system provides all the detailed information QuickBooks needs for reporting. But what if your QuickBooks data is inaccurate? This is why I recommend that you reconcile QuickBooks to your POS. Doing so ensures that nothing was missed. So, even if you were tired on the third Wednesday of the month and forgot to enter sales, reconciling your sales ensures that items are not missed and are resolved every month.

CREDIT CARD RECEIVABLE RECONCILIATION

Like most restaurants, although you take credit cards daily, they are processed every few days in what are called batches. I set up this book to have you create a credit card receivable account to ensure that you receive all the monies from the credit card processor that you think you've received. At the end of every month, you need to reconcile this account to ensure that you have in fact received all the monies and that the amounts pending are correct. I go further into this in Chapter 13.

CASH ON HAND RECONCILIATION

Cash on hand, one of the biggest challenges for most restaurant owners, is always a tough current asset to track. At least 25 percent of your sales often come in cash, and for certain markets this could be substantially higher. Cash, more often than not, does not always end up where it is supposed to. That is why reconciling this account on a monthly basis is so crucial to your success: It helps to ensure that you actually have all the cash you think you have.

If the account does not reconcile, this gives you the opportunity to figure out where the cash went. If it was used for a purchase, make sure to record those receipts.

OTHER CURRENT ASSET RECONCILIATION

All businesses are not the same: This means that you may have other current assets on your balance sheet. These balances fluctuate and should be reconciled to some version of back up, be it a ledger or statement.

REVIEW PAYROLL ENTRIES

Restaurant payroll is often one of the largest costs and biggest time sucks for restaurant owners and operators. You must ensure that payroll taxes, tips, and wages hit the income statement and balance sheet correctly, that net checks are recorded properly on the balance sheet and much more. This does not even include the proper recording and entry of hours for hourly employees to ensure the paychecks are accurate.

I dove into this in Chapter 7, but it is important to mention it here again. At the end of the month, it is crucial that you, the owner (or your accountant), perform a quick review of payroll entries to ensure that they are accurate. Make sure that the payroll journals post correctly, net checks are zeroed out on the balance sheet, tips payable is reconciling properly, and that wages for departments are recorded on the correct line items on the balance sheet.

MONTHLY ACCRUALS

An accrual is a journal entry that is used to recognize revenues and expenses that have been earned or used within a period. Accruals are necessary to ensure that all revenues and expenses are recognized within the correct reporting period, irrespective of the timing of the related cash flows.

Under the double-entry bookkeeping system, an accrued expense is offset by a liability, which appears in a line item in the balance sheet. If accrued revenue is recorded, it is offset by an asset, such as unbilled service fees, which also appears as a line item in the balance sheet.

Some popular accruals in the restaurant world are payroll and insurance.

I covered payroll accruals in Chapter 7 when I discussed payroll. Below I will cover a simple insurance accrual to help you better understand how to make these adjustments.

Let's look at an example. George's restaurant purchased a 1-year insurance policy for $1200. The journal entry on Feb. 1 was:

ACCOUNT	DEBIT	CREDIT
1400 - Prepaid Expenses (Insurance)	$1,200	
1010 - Bank Account		$1,200
Total	$1,200	$1,200

This is the same as booking the expense to prepaid insurance.

At the end of February, one month's insurance has been used. The monthly portion of insurance is $100, therefore $100 must be removed from the asset account, Prepaid Expenses (Insurance) and transferred to the expense account, Insurance Expense. This adjusting entry will match the expenses incurred in February with the revenues received in February.

ACCOUNT	DEBIT	CREDIT
7030 - Insurance Expense	$100	
1400 - Prepaid Expenses (Insurance)		$100
Total	$100	$100

The above is how to record the insurance expense for February.

LINE ITEM REVIEW

Of course, you should know your business inside and out. To ensure that everything is correct and accurate, you should do an in-depth review of your balance sheet and profit and loss statement (although these reports are combined in the general ledger, reviewing the general ledger can be a bit confusing for a newbie). Pull these reports within the QuickBooks software, and review each line item. Do these income items belong here? Do these expenses belong here? Is this invoice from a vendor for cleaning supplies or food cost of goods? This is a very important step in the financial preparation and monthly close process. Making sure everything is accurate and true at this step will result in fewer headaches down the road.

Not sure how to class something? Well, make sure to shoot your CPA an email because a good CPA knows that helping you now will make their life easier in March.

The review should not stop at ensuring each item is classified correctly but should also ensure items are in the correct period. At the end of the month, are all the invoices truly for that period? You do not want to have your previous month look like a mess and your current month look great if that is just not true. Proper accounting should flush out large variances unless large variances are the nature of your business.

PREPARE FINANCIALS

Once you are confident with all the transactions across the period, you can prepare financial statements. Usually this report is prepared for the previous financial month. It includes the profit and loss statement, balance sheet, and cash flow statement.

I will dive deeper into this in the next chapter.

MANAGEMENT REVIEW

A good leader ensures that everyone is on the same page. The management review of financials also ensures everything is in its right place. By reviewing financials with your management team, you can ensure that invoices did not slip through the cracks and that random payments did not go out when they weren't supposed to. Additionally, a good management team knows their rough margins. So, active discussions around the operating metrics ensure that the financials are accurate and that your team can respond to challenges as they appear rather months later—this type of proactive versus reactive problem solving is the key to success. It also helps ensure that all vendors are coded correctly, and it's a great opportunity to get your management team involved.

CLOSE THE PERIOD

The last and probably most important step in the monthly close process is ensuring that no one makes changes to the agreed-upon financials after they have been modified for the last time. To do this, simply close the accounting period. This is a simple option in the QuickBooks Desktop under Settings, and for QBO users under Company Settings and then under Advanced Settings. The period close date should be set to the last day of the previous month, and a password should be set. Generate that password and save it somewhere, but don't share it with your team! If this password is shared with your team, then they can make changes to previous periods where you may have already presented financials.

CLOSING THE PERIOD IN QUICKBOOKS DESKTOP

1) From the home screen, select Edit from the top navigation bar.
2) Then from the drop-down, select Preferences and then Accounting.
3) From the navigation in the middle of the screen, select Company Preferences.
4) Then select Set Date/Password.
5) From the pop-up, select a closing date and password (if only one person is working within QuickBooks, there is no need to set the password).
6) Choose OK to accept and close the window.

CLOSING THE PERIOD IN QUICKBOOKS ONLINE

1) From the home screen, select the gear icon from the top right of the screen.
2) Under Your Company, select Account and Settings.
3) From the menu located on the left side of the screen, select Advanced.
4) Select the pencil icon in the Accounting section.
5) Choose the Close the Books checkbox.
6) Enter a closing date and password if preferred.
7) Select save, and then done.

CREATE A CHECKLIST!

Every company is different and has different financial needs. The reality is the above checklist may not be inclusive of everything you need to close your month, or it may be too in-depth. Only you will know what is right for your business, so you should consult with your CPA if you are not quite sure.

The smoothest way to ensure you cover all the necessary items mentioned above is to create a simple checklist in Excel, with a section for notes, to use each month. You should use a fresh checklist every month. The checklist helps guide your month close process, but it can also help you troubleshoot. For example, in the hurry of getting the books closed, you may have forgotten to do something, or you may need to make a change the following month. By reviewing your relevant checklist, you will ensure that issues do not plague you right up until it is time to file taxes and are instead handled in a timely fashion.

ORGANIZING THE MONTH CLOSE

If you are a stickler for organization, I recommend that you find a digital place to house all your information. You could, for instance, place the files on a computer that you back up regularly, or on a cloud-based storage service, or on an external hard drive. This device or service should be organized by year and then month. All your items for, say, June should be stored within that June folder.

Using this type of organization system makes it easier to report to investors and share with your accountant and/or business partners. Everything will be closed properly, and any changes will be backed up.

Included in this backup hub should be everything that you marked off the previously mentioned checklist—everything from your POS reports to your reconciliation of loans. Don't stop there, though, include all your loan statements, bank statements, and anything else pertaining to the month. In the world of accounting and keeping a paper trail, more is always better!

USE AN EXPERT'S CHECKLIST

Sometimes the first version of a monthly close checklist can be daunting. Lucky for you I went ahead and created one for your use! Head over to my website zacweiner.com and simply search for "monthly close checklist"—you will be able to easily download an Excel sample version.

CONCLUSION

This is one of the chapters that I easily admit can be overwhelming. However, try to imagine a scenario when you do not handle all the above related items on a monthly basis, but instead rush to get them all done in January before tax season. Many small business owners end up in this boat, and it makes them dread and despise accounting even more. I recommend that you take the previous chapter to heart and understand that the more you do every month throughout the year, the more in control and the less overwhelmed you will be by your business during the first of the year.

13

RECONCILIATION

RECONCILIATIONS: PRIORITY ONE

What's the main activity most everyone who runs a small business skips when it comes to accounting? Reconciliations! Avoidance may seem like a good tactic because reconciliations can seem pointless. Yes, I remember the first time I had to do a reconciliation: I wondered why I had to check over all the work I had already completed. Isn't it a waste of time? Well, when you're reporting financials, filing taxes, or doing anything that has real-world ramifications, double-checking your work is vital to your long-term wellbeing. It may be a hard at first, but with this chapter and a little bit of practice, you will be a reconciliation master in no time.

RESTAURANT RECONCILIATIONS ARE DIFFERENT

For restaurants, reconciliations take on a life of their own, one in which they are incredibly important. Their priority exists for a few reasons: One, even a small café deals with thousands of dollars in cash (so you better know where your cash is); two, I've said it before and I'll say it again, cash flow is everything. You reconcile to account for all your cash. To ensure the bank balances represented in QuickBooks are accurate, you must reconcile. This chapter serves to give you both the tools and error-tracking ability to reconcile efficiently and accurately. It may still seem like a burden, but doesn't the burden of reconciling outweigh any amount of missing cash?

WHAT IS RECONCILING?

In layman's terms, reconciling means providing verification that an account balance is correct. For example, I reconcile the balance in the checking account to the balance shown on the bank statement. In the context of a restaurant, the objective is to report the correct amount in your checking account chart of accounts within QuickBooks. By reconciling this account, you ensure that you did not miss that crazy bank fee or post a mistaken amount to the account. You also ensure that you weren't overcharged by a vendor.

The Generally Accepted Accounting Principles (GAAP) are a set of accounting principles, procedures, and standards that organizations use in order to compile their financial statements. GAAP is essentially the rulebook by which the accounting community lives by. Generally Accepted Accounting Principles state that the purpose of account reconciliation is to provide accuracy and consistency in financial accounts. To ensure all cash outlays and inlays match between cash flow statements and income statements, it is necessary to carry out reconciliation accounts.

As you become more experienced within QuickBooks, you may come to find making sales entries and paying bills is a fun and exciting activity. You will use this information to make business decisions and move your enterprise forward. How do you ensure that the information on hand is correct? That is where reconciling comes in—it ensures that all the transactions in your reports are correct and true to form.

Reconciliation is a process that will benefit your restaurant because it helps avoid errors that may have detrimental ramifications. Do you really want to give your business partner a report showing you made money when you didn't? In the world of business, your word is everything. If your financials are based on your word, but those financials are incorrect, well, unfortunately, your word is incorrect. Reconciliation also plays a valuable role in helping against fraud and ensuring financial integrity.

Additionally, reconciliations help you spot checks that haven't cleared from months before. Is this vendor still owed money? Was it a duplicated transaction? If so, it needs to be removed, and your financial statements need to be redone. Ultimately, reconciling helps you spot errors and ensures that you fix them in a timely fashion.

Additionally, reconciling plays an important role in ensuring that all your money is where it is supposed to be. For example, perhaps you take credit card payments through one of the popular POS systems, or you deposit cash weekly at the bank. Oftentimes your credit card processor forgets to batch your money, and sometimes your bank forgets to apply deposits to your account. As crazy as it might sound, it happens all the time—to the tune of hundreds of thousands of dollars. I have seen it firsthand—reconciling ensures that those errors are caught well before you need the money.

WHAT EXACTLY SHOULD I RECONCILE?

Below is a list of all the accounts you should reconcile and a short background on why they are important.

BANK ACCOUNT

As you have now surely realized, reconciling is of the utmost importance. There are multiple accounts that should be reconciled on a monthly basis to ensure the accuracy of your accounting. The most important of these is the bank account.

Restaurants live and breathe by cash flow or cash on hand. If no cash is on hand, no bills can be paid. If no bills can be paid, employees can't be paid, food inventory can't be purchased, rent can't be paid, and the doors close.

QuickBooks gives you an account balance in the bank account based on the transactions within QuickBooks. When you cut checks, you surely cut checks so that the balance does not fall below zero. If you have payroll or a tax liability due in the near future, you need to be sure that the checks you cut now *plus* future payables do not fall below that dreaded zero mark.

For those of you with multiple bank accounts—for example, a payroll clearing account, a sales tax liability account, multiple checking accounts for various locations, and so on—reconciling all bank accounts where money is held should be your number one priority on a monthly basis.

Reconciling your bank accounts serves an additional purpose rarely mentioned. Reconciling these accounts on a regular basis ensures you are protected from fraud. Fraud of all types occurs in the world of business. Perhaps someone got hold of a check or your debit card. By reconciling your account on a regular basis, you protect yourself from letting these transactions go unnoticed. Your prompt awareness of these occurrences enables you to react in a timely fashion—by canceling cards or transferring to a new account with new account numbers.

LIABILITIES

Liabilities, liabilities, liabilities: They are the root of small business failure. Leverage and debt are great for growing your small business because they allow you to use less of your own capital to get outsized returns. But these liabilities are often due on a monthly basis. This means that the outstanding balance must be correct before payment is due.

CREDIT CARDS

Most restaurants will give management employees credit cards because these employees wear many hats—often running to the store to pick up some produce, grabbing some forgotten bar mixer, making an online purchase, etc. It is vital to ensure that each credit card is reconciled and that there are no nasty surprises hidden away. You want to know in advance if an employee went Christmas shopping on your card!

As mentioned previously, fraud is a major issue when it comes to credit cards, so by ensuring the credit card balances are correct, you ensure that your business metrics are correct. By reconciling your account, you are positive that the charges are correct, and when any surprises arise, you find out right away and can get to the root of the cause.

RECEIVABLES

Most restaurants that operate today accept credit cards and likely have a payment processor that deposits every few days. This is considered a receivable, and you want to ensure that you receive all the money that is rightfully yours when you are supposed to.

Booking accurate sales in your system is very important but only half the battle. More important than booking the correct sale is ensuring you get your money. A simple receivable reconciliation can be performed on a weekly or monthly basis.

Credit card processors or POS systems sometimes hold back money or don't deposit the correct amount. It is your job as the business owner to ensure all the right amounts are deposited. I have occasionally even seen processors forget to make deposits or hold back money for some wild reason that takes faxing over paperwork to resolve. Regardless of the circumstance, by reconciling your receivables you can ensure that you are getting all the money that is rightfully yours.

PRO TIP

Remember to add an expense into your credit card receivable account for processing fees. If these are not included the receivable account will not balance.

PAYABLES

Like the many other accounts that need to be reconciled, you must ensure that your payables number matches that of your payables on your balance sheet. This can be a bit confusing at first, but overall you want the bills you have to pay to show up properly in your accounts payable.

Before closing the books at the end of each reporting period, you must verify that the detailed total of all accounts payable outstanding matches the payables account balance stated in the general ledger. Doing so ensures that the amount of accounts payable reported in the balance sheet is correct. This is called an accounts payable reconciliation.

This reconciliation process can be a difficult one when performed for the first time. However, once all errors have been spotted and corrections made, it is usually relatively easy to update the reconciliation document in subsequent reporting periods.

CASH ON HAND

The hard cash that you receive on a daily basis is referred to as petty cash or cash on hand. You might sometimes pay small bills out of this, or large ones if you frequently deal in cash. These are all business expenses, and it is your job to track these transactions. That is where reconciling cash on hand comes in—reconciling allows you to account for all your cash expenditures.

For moderate- to large-sized restaurants, 20 percent or more of your revenue might be transacted in cash. The more cash is transacted, the more likely some cash is to disappear—this is just the nature of dealing with large numbers. Reconciling cash on hand along with depositing cash weekly will ensure that small variances are resolved before they turn into big variances.

BEFORE YOU RECONCILE

Before you reconcile your accounts, check these things:

1) Be sure you are up-to-date on entering your transactions in QuickBooks.
2) Enter all transactions that have not cleared or shown up on bank statements that you will be reconciling (checks or bill payments).
3) Update your bank feed to a date past the ending period of your statements. This ensures that you captured all transactions during the period.
4) Print all statements or pull them up on a dual monitor setup with a pdf modifier.

PRO TIP

The very first time you reconcile, check the opening balance transaction on your bank accounts in your QuickBooks chart of accounts. This should reflect the amount that was actually in your account when you began using QuickBooks. If it doesn't match, you can fix this by following the below steps:

In your QuickBooks chart of accounts, open the register for the account (double-click the account name) and change the opening balance transaction (which is usually the first transaction that appears within the register) to match the ending balance from the last bank statement you received before you started using QuickBooks.

Most importantly, before you reconcile your accounts, be sure to have all your ducks in a row. Have your statements printed, a hot coffee in hand, your pen, and a comfy chair. The first time you do this will be challenging, but I promise it gets easier from here.

HOW DO I RECONCILE?

QUICKBOOKS DESKTOP (ALL VERSIONS)

QuickBooks Desktop makes reconciliation a bit more challenging than QuickBooks Online (described below), or maybe just more unfriendly to the eyes. To begin your reconciliation, visit the

Banking menu and select Reconcile (this option also exists on the home screen, labeled Reconcile).

You will then be prompted to select which account you would like to reconcile, as I discussed above. You should enter your account's ending balance in the ending balance section along with the ending date as mentioned above. Then, you click Continue to begin the reconciliation.

At this point, you should check items as they appear on your bank account statement. As you work down the bank statement (checking those items as selected in QuickBooks with your pen), your difference amount should approach zero, and when your difference is zero and all the monthly items listed on your bank statement are included, congrats! You can click Reconcile Now, and the reconciliation is complete.

As mentioned above, it is also important that all transactions for the period have been marked off of your statement. If you have a deposit showing on your bank statement but not in your QuickBooks account, that is a no-no. Figure out why this transaction appears or does not appear. Ensure all transactions have been selected in QuickBooks that are on your bank statement and that your ending balance is correct.

QUICKBOOKS ONLINE
QuickBooks Online makes reconciliations a breeze. First, you must navigate to the Reconcile menu. To do this, simply start at the home screen, click on the Gear icon in the top right, and beneath the column heading Tools, select the Reconcile tab.

The next step is probably your most important—which account

will you reconcile? It is important to reconcile all the accounts that I highlight in this chapter. Depending on how your business is set up, it is most beneficial to reconcile receivables, cash on hand, and credit cards prior to your bank account. This helps ensure you track complex errors before doing your bank reconciliation, so you do not have to redo it. Choose the account you want to reconcile from the drop-down menu options (all the accounts are explained at the end of the chapter). Once you've selected your account, click Reconcile Now.

Now you must enter your statement details. For bank statements, you just need to enter the end date and ending amount. For items like receivables, cash on hand, etc. you can enter $0 or the actual ending amount. Let's say you have $400 in the cash register draw, that should be your beginning or ending balance. You could also pretend like the $400 does not exist and count based off of $0 for the beginning and ending amounts.

Now the real work begins. Take another look at the transaction history on your bank statement. In the Reconcile window, match each transaction from your bank statement with an item in the list, checking the box to the right of each transaction to match and denoting it on the bank statement with a pen mark. If you are reconciling other accounts like receivables, just ensure that your outflows match your inflows. For example, if you booked $1,000 in sales on the 5th, you should see that deposit on the 8th.

Now you can finish your reconciliation. When you've gotten the difference value at the bottom to zero you are all set. Though it is important to understand that you don't just want a zero ending balance, but rather you want all your transactions that are checked to match those on your statement with a zero ending balance.

Clearing transactions for next month while working on last month's bank statements makes no sense!

It is also important that all transactions for the period have been marked off of your statement. If there's a deposit on your bank statement but not in your QuickBooks account, there's a problem. Figure out why this transaction appears or does not appear. Then, ensure all transactions have been selected in QuickBooks that are on your bank statement and that your ending balance is correct.

FIXING BROKEN RECONCILIATIONS

There will be times when you will have worked diligently to update your QuickBooks—adding all the transactions, writing checks out of the system, matching everything to the correct general ledger code—but can't seem to make your reconciliations work.

Well, here are a few potential reasons your reconciliations are broken:

1) You changed something in a previous period that affects a current reconciliation.
2) You are missing transactions from a current reconciliation that needs to be added in.
3) You entered transactions or wrote checks from the wrong account in QuickBooks.

RESOLVING A PREVIOUS PERIOD ISSUE

Compare the ending account balance in the general ledger for the immediately preceding period to the starting amount in your reconciliation window. Do they match? If these numbers do not match, you will have to reconcile earlier periods before attempting to reconcile the current period.

QuickBooks has a feature called Locate Discrepancies. This should help you find the transaction that was changed, deleted, or added. Take a look at the report and see if the transactions remind you of a previous transaction that exists, does not exist, or that may have been entered multiple times.

For beginners, it might be best, if it is a recent reconciliation, to undo your previous reconciliation and redo it. Yes, it's a bit more work, but you want your books to be accurate. Ideally, after you redo the reconciliation and add or remove the culprit transaction, your reconciliation will be ready to go for the current period.

RESOLVING MISSING TRANSACTIONS

Sometimes you will get busy during the month and forget to add a debit that was made at the gas station or sales from a certain day. This is normal and happens to the best of us—it is the reason why you reconcile.

You will want to go through your reconciliations, for example with the bank statement, circling items that are missing from your QuickBooks. Then, once you get to the end of the reconciliation using the Find feature in QuickBooks Desktop (Edit » Find) or the search bar in QuickBooks Online, you will search for those missing amounts. Maybe you entered them but entered them incorrectly. Perhaps you used the checking account but accidentally said you used cash on hand or vice versa.

If you are out of luck and the transactions are nowhere to be found, then it is likely you missed entering them, so go to your check register and enter the missing transactions. To access your check register for a specific account, locate your chart of accounts and double click the account (such as Checking Bank) that is missing the transactions. Now when you reopen your reconciliation window those transactions will be there for you to match to your statements, bringing your totals right where they need to be!

RESOLVING TRANSACTIONS FROM THE WRONG ACCOUNT

I mentioned this a bit earlier, but sometimes when you're in a hurry you may write checks, make deposits, or enter expenses incorrectly within QuickBooks. All this means is that you selected the wrong drop-down when performing a certain activity like the one mentioned above. For example, did you enter a checking account expense into your savings account?

To resolve this issue, simply revisit the individual transactions. QuickBooks is great because it has drop-down features that let you select which account you would like to print a check from. If you accidentally selected savings but meant checking, simply select the other account from the drop-down.

Most restaurants have light activity in their savings accounts. This means if you accidentally used the incorrect bank account for a transaction, spotting those problem transactions is a breeze! Simply open the account register for your savings and viola, the transaction will be right there.

To put these transactions in the right account, delete them from the wrong account and reenter them in the correct account. When you reconcile at the end of the month, you know you performed it correctly when everything matches!

OTHER RECONCILIATION ISSUES

MISTAKENLY CLEARING TRANSACTIONS NOT ON STATEMENT
I do it, and you will do it, too: When I'm rushing to mark all the transactions on a reconciliation, sometimes I mismark the wrong one. If you can't easily pinpoint which transaction you incorrectly marked, simply start fresh—a bit of a pain, but get it right the first time and avoid trouble down the road.

NOT MARKING ALL TRANSACTIONS SHOWN ON STATEMENT
Sure, I can make the reconciliation balance—selecting nothing ensures a $0 variance. However, the point of reconciliations is to ensure that all transactions you think occurred actually occurred. Make sure you mark all transactions shown on your statement!

CONFIRM BEGINNING BALANCE
I touched on this a bit above, but when you make a change in a previous period, the beginning balance will be inaccurate. That means you need to pinpoint where you incorrectly made a historical change and repair it.

CONFIRM ENDING BALANCE
Often in the heat of the moment when you are in a hurry, you may mistype something. This could be shortchanging the ending balance by a mere 10 cents or perhaps even a few dollars. This small difference will always throw off the balance, but it is an easy fix. This is as simply as putting a 5 in the last space instead of a 4. Simply edit your reconciliation info and fix the error.

CONCLUSION

Most of us hated tests growing up, particularly because they tend to be pointless. Reconciliations are a test that serve a real purpose, to verify that the information entered into the accounting system is accurate and true. Most business owners that receive financials never question if they are accurate and true, so ensure your reconciliations are complete and that your assumptions are true. Accounting in the basic context is the concept of checks and balances and that is why reconciliations are important. So, take the time to ensure your reconciliations are completed monthly. It will pay dividends with accurate financials.

14
RESTAURANT REPORTS AND FINANCIAL STATEMENTS

FINANCIALS

As I mentioned at the start of the book, accounting serves two major purposes; One, it serves as the reporting method by which small businesses comply with local and federal tax laws (aka, it helps ensure you pay your taxes), and two, it serves as the method by which you report the businesses financial performance to owners and partners. This chapter serves to guide all your restaurant reporting needs, from month and quarter ending financials to weekly and biweekly reports that will help you drive business performance. The previous parts of this book were essentially devised to educate you on the thoughts, processes, and procedures to execute and review items in this coming chapter. Think about it like this: If most of this book consisted of weekly quizzes, the financial chapter is your final.

RESTAURANT FINANCIALS

Restaurant financials are similar to most other small business financials, they should include a profit and loss statement, balance sheet statement along with a statement of cash flows. Not exactly sure what these are? No need to worry because I'm about to go over them. The main difference between other business and restaurants is that in restaurants, fluctuations can occur week to week. That is why in this chapter I suggest implementing some other key metrics and reporting, such as weekly flash reports. Why not track and adjust to weekly business fluctuations before the month is already complete?

Additionally, I point out restaurant-specific metrics to focus on for your regular reporting, such as how to run some very quick and easy custom reporting within QuickBooks to quickly create high-level reporting.

THE MAIN FINANCIAL REPORTS

Three reports are the lifeblood of your monthly, quarterly, and annual business financial reporting:

1) Profit and loss statement
2) Balance sheet
3) Statement of cash flows

PROFIT AND LOSS STATEMENT (INCOME STATEMENT)

This report is an overview of income and expenses for a specific period of time. Additionally, you can quickly see if business performance is on track and what recent initiatives are succeeding or failing. The profit and loss statement shows income earned under the accrual method. It will show all invoices that have been issued, sales recorded, journals entered, and so on. These items will be included even if there are no cash expenditures or money received for them. So even though you have recorded an invoice, you may not have been paid for it yet.

Many business owners confuse the profit and loss profitability (net income) with cash the business has made: It is possible to show profits and have reduced cash flow in the same period, unless your business is totally run on a cash basis. For example, this may happen when you purchase fixed assets. A fixed asset, like a new oven, is shown on the balance sheet. It is not an expense on the income statement, though the cash still left the business. This report shows you whether you are making money or not based on the activity of the business during the period.

HOW TO REVIEW THE PROFIT AND LOSS STATEMENT
I recommend looking at the monthly view, quarterly view, and

then the quarterly broken out in the monthly format. By reviewing against previous months, you will better see any anomalies.

Additionally, I recommend reviewing a few points for your business:

1) Year-over-year sales for the period. This could be the week, month or quarter. Often restaurants are afflicted with seasonality, so reviewing your reports for the same time period this year versus last year will ensure you are taking into account seasonality within your business. Is your business growing? If not, why? Is one department, food or beverage growing? If not, why?

2) Prime costs as a percentage of sales. Look at your total food and beverage costs relative to sales, along with your total payroll expenditure—depending on your market and business setup—they both should be around 30 to 35 percent. For example, some quick service restaurants may have higher food costs but a lower payroll expense. (The quick trick is to simply run your profit and loss statement, select Customize Report, and select Show Percentages.)

3) Review other major and minor expenses. Take a look at all your expense line items, specifically rent, insurance, and utilities first. Are these inline to prior months? How are they as a percentage of sales relative to other periods? If fluctuations occur, what is causing them?

Though it may feel like quite a few questions to answer, the point is to start having a dialogue with your business. What caused the current business performance? Can you change the results for the next period? What can you do to reduce this expense? Through regular review, you can build the framework to push your business forward.

The other facet to an income statement review is to understand that multiple small transactions are compiled to create the number presented in the final report. So, review the detailed ledger of smaller transactions, find out if a particular transaction is the culprit of the issue. Dial down as it were, because sometimes the problem is in the weeds.

⏱ **30-SECOND REVIEW ITEMS**
In a hurry? Here are the three things you should review if you only have 30 seconds:

1) *Review top line income because this measure most directly affects net income.*
2) *Review cost of goods sold (or prime costs) to review margins.*
3) *Review net income (as a total number and percentage of sales).*

BALANCE SHEET

The balance sheet shows a financial picture of a business on a specific day. It runs down the assets (what the company owns), its liabilities (what it owes), and the difference between those two, or the company's equity. Some noteworthy line items on the balance sheet include: cash, accounts receivable, inventory, accounts payable, and (if you have debt), the portion of long-term debt that is due this year and the balance of any short-term loans (usually secured by accounts receivable and inventory).

You can quickly get the feeling for the health of the business by comparing current assets to current liabilities. For example, do you owe more in accounts payable than you have in receivables and cash? Is so, you have a problem! The balance sheet allows you to see what you owe against what you have very quickly, highlighting pain points before they occur.

Over time, a comparison of period-ending balance sheets can give a good picture of the financial health of your business. In conjunction with other financial statements, it forms the basis for sophisticated analysis of your business. The balance sheet is also a tool to evaluate a company's current flexibility and liquidity.

Additionally, I recommend reviewing a few points for your business:

1) Review the businesses assets, most importantly your current assets. Do you have enough cash in the bank to cover current payables (sales tax included)? Is your business accumulating cash month over month? Specifically to restaurants, is all your cash on hand getting deposited? Are those balances correct relative to your normal standards?

2) Review your current inventory. Unlike most other small businesses, your restaurant inventory spoils if not used. Ensure that you are maintaining normal inventory balances for both food and beverage. Recommended amounts are 30 days of on-hand inventory, so take a look at last month's cost of goods from your income statement; see if it is in line with your current on-hand inventory. If it is higher, adjust, because you have dollars that could be in your pocket that are instead sitting in your freezer and fridge.

3) Review your liabilities. Specifically, ensure you have enough assets to cover your liabilities. Does your sales tax look correct for the average monthly sales? Is accounts

payables (unpaid bills) in line from month to month?
Are other company debts being serviced such as lines of
credits, credit cards and notes payable? Always remember
that a healthy business is one that pays its bills on time!

4) Review your equity. Equity is the current net worth of the
business. Owners draws and distributions are reported
in this area of the balance sheet. This area also includes
historical profits and losses (called retained earnings) and
this year's profits and losses, denoted as net income.

The balance sheet offers a picture of true financial health on a set
day. Think about it in simple terms, like taking your temperature.
Though you may not feel great, without an increase in temperature, it is probably nothing to be alarmed over. Similar with the
balance sheet, sometimes payables and cash fluctuate both up and
down: Unless there is a significant negative trend over a few periods, there is nothing to be alarmed over.

That said, the balance sheet is a great place to see how the day-
to-day business actions reported in the income statement have a
more long-term impact on financial health. Make sure the positive
decisions you are making in response to your income statement
reporting are reflected in your balance sheet.

You will find that in the balance sheet arena, I avoided referencing
any specific percentages. In fact, your balance sheet health report
is really specific to your business. Just ensure you have the working
capital (readily available cash) to cover debts today, next week, and
into the future.

⏱ **30-SECOND REVIEW ITEMS**

In a hurry? Here are the three things you should review if you only have 30 seconds:

1) *Review large changes in asset and liabilities. (The balance sheet month over month report is perfect for this.)*
2) *Calculate and track your current ratio (current ratio equals current assets divided by current liabilities).*
3) *Calculate and track working capital (working capital equals total current assets minus total current liabilities).*

STATEMENT OF CASH FLOWS

This is a summary of money received and payments made during the period. This may include investing activities as well as financing activities. In layman's terms, this means that if you borrowed money, accrued expenses, distributed money to partners, paid sales tax, and so on, these items will be highlighted in this report. I find the statement of cash flows the most insightful report out of all three main financial reports.

Why such a valuable report? Mostly because it is totally binary—a simple yes or no—and an indication of success or failure. Did the business accumulate additional capital over the period or squander it? If it used or accumulated, this report will clearly show the former or latter. I find this report the true testament of the business's performance for the period. The goal of all restaurants I have been associated with is to make money, as measured by the profits available to be distributed to the owners, and this report clearly shows if that is happening and if not, where to focus your energy to make it happen.

By showing what is happening in the cash position today, this month, or last quarter, you can see the pain points in the business. For example, are net profits strong but owner's distributions too high? Are accounts receivable continuing to grow month after month? Is the business profitable but inventory continuing to grow? Lots of insight can be taken from this short report.

⏱ 30-SECOND REVIEW ITEMS

In a hurry? Here are the three things you should review if you only have 30 seconds:

1) *Aim for a positive cash flow from operations.*
2) *Keep a close eye on accounts receivable (hint: it shouldn't be growing unless your business is substantially growing).*
3) *Plan ahead for cash crunches.*
4) *Growing inventory should mean growing sales. If not, adjust quickly.*
5) *Understand the difference between profit and cash, and—more importantly—what is causing the divergence.*

DAILY, WEEKLY, AND BIWEEKLY REPORTING

Yes, reviewing up-to-date and accurate financials as outlined previously in the chapter is very valuable to understanding and better operating your business. Though the main issue with those reports is that they are always reflective, by multiple weeks. They are always backwards looking, meaning your time to react based on that information is minimal. By reviewing key metrics on a daily, weekly, and biweekly basis, you can make adjustments on the fly, meaning positive changes can be implemented prior to monthly reporting, hopefully ensuring better business performance and related financial reporting.

DAILY RESTAURANT SALES

Understanding what is happening in your business on a daily and weekly basis helps restaurant owners and operators achieve long-term success. The daily sales report can help provide this picture. This could come directly from the POS or simply be a customized Excel report taken from raw sales data. Either way, understanding the sales flow of your business will help you spot trends before they become an issue.

One of my favorite examples of this is the restaurant that is open seven days a week. Every Monday sales are abysmal, 1/20th of a normal day in sales. By looking at the financials in a monthly aggregate format, one would not notice the reduced sales specifically on Monday. Rather they simply see cost of goods and labor elevated for the entirety of the month. By looking at financials daily, however, the owner or operator sees the Monday trend over the monthly period, realizes they are spending more money on labor every Monday than gaining in sales, and decides to close for Monday, which drives more revenue to the bottom line every month into the future.

🕐 **30-SECOND REVIEW ITEMS**
In a hurry? Here are the three things you should review if you only have 30 seconds:

1) *Daily income*
2) *Profit center percentage of total*

DAILY LABOR ANALYSIS

For restaurants, the daily labor expense is vital to success or failure. Life is mostly not binary, but when it comes to restaurant labor, this is usually the largest expense for any restaurant. Knowing these numbers daily, and tracking their fluctuations, gives you time to react before you are unable to cover your weekly payroll expense.

This analysis is a simple report that maps out what your labor cost is by department or profit center and that shows the main expenses. Don't forget to include your salaried and management employees because the business still needs to pay for them, too (the trick here is to take their annual salary and simply divide by 365; although they may not work 7 days a week, their salary should be amortized over the working week in that manner to give you an accurate depiction).

By reviewing this item daily, you can see the relevant fluctuations and how they impact your business. Even if your business remains consistently steady, you can ensure that you are making a strong profit by adding this into your daily review. Using this report in conjunction with your daily sales will help you figure out your labor margin, which is important for labor intensive businesses or even those with a large overhead management.

⏱ 30-SECOND REVIEW ITEMS
In a hurry? Here are the three things you should review if you only have 30 seconds:

1) *Daily labor gross dollar amoun*
2) *Department percentage of total*
3) *Fixed and variable percentage of total*

PRO TIP

Combine the daily sales, daily labor, and the estimated monthly fixed cost (rent and insurance divided by the number of days in the month). Now you can track your daily profitability in the matter of minutes, no longer waiting weeks to know how your performance is doing!

RESTAURANT WEEKLY FLASH REPORT

As I highlighted earlier in the chapter, the profit and loss report highlighting company profitability for a period of time is a crucial report for knowing more about your business's performance. What if I said that same report could be broken out weekly? That's right, the weekly flash report mimics your regular profit and loss statement but helps you keep tabs on your business on a weekly basis. Though this report may not be one hundred percent precise due to monthly invoices or accruals or simply missed data entry, you will likely get a strong feel for what is happening week to week.

By reviewing main items from week to week, you can see if items like labor, sales, and other controllable expenses are falling in line. This report also gives you the ability to address things before the month is completed and make key changes before any problems spiral out of control.

⏱ 30-SECOND REVIEW ITEMS

In a hurry? Here are the three things you should review if you only have 30 seconds:

1) *Weekly profitability*
2) *Operating margins*
3) *Week-over-week operating margins*

WEEKLY UNPAID BILLS REPORT

Knowing who you owe and how much you owe them is as important as knowing where and how much in sales has been generated. Hopefully you are entering invoices on a weekly basis, as referenced in a few other places within this book. If not, you should start now.

Once all the invoices are entered, perhaps even before you make your weekly check run, review your unpaid bills report! This report will show all vendors, relevant invoices, and what is owed on those invoices.

This report is more important than most restaurant owners and operators realize, for one simple reason: Reviewing this report allows you to be proactive. In layman's terms, you can see what you owe in advance. Instead of realizing that today you owe Vendor A $15,000 and Vendor B $15,000 and have $100 in the bank, you see those expenses weeks in advance and can manage your cash flow properly. The Weekly Unpaid Bills report allows you to be proactive versus reactive, which is the mark of a successful business owner.

⏱ 30-SECOND REVIEW ITEMS

In a hurry? Here are the three things you should review if you only have 30 seconds:

1) *Week-over-week increase or decrease*
2) *Current liquidity*

WEEKLY ACCOUNTS RECEIVABLE REPORT (FOR CATERERS)

As important as knowing what you owe is knowing who owes you money. Most restaurants deposits are fairly automatic, and you should have limited issues with receivables outlined in the sales chapter (since you reconcile receivable accounts regularly). Though caterers have an entirely different element that they must be aware of, which is that customers are sometimes extended credit, and this must be followed up on.

Keeping a finger on the pulse of who owes you money is fundamental to managing your cash flow. This ensures that you know when money is coming in and you know when to apply leverage to ensure that you keep overdue accounts current. Additionally, it allows you to react quickly to long-time customers who are behind and to easily send a note about overdue amounts.

Effective management of accounts receivable will have direct positive impacts on your cash flow. Essentially, accounts receivable is money that just needs to be turned into cash. The quicker you turn it into cash the better your business cash flow. So focus on this weekly to ensure you are ahead of the curve.

⏱ 30-SECOND REVIEW ITEMS

In a hurry? Here are the three things you should review if you only have 30 seconds:

1) *Week-over-week increase or decrease*
2) *Overdue accounts and their current balance*

CONCLUSION

Financials and reports are not simply at the end of this book because they have less value than the other information. No, they are located at the end because everything else outlined in this book allows for these financials and reports to be accurate and true. The methodologies and approaches outlined throughout this book allow you to run a simple report, review accurate information and make an educated decision. Leverage these reports to better run your business.

15

GOODBYE

CONGRATULATIONS

The easy part is now done, now it's time to implement what you've learned.

Restaurant owners are challenged from all sides the first moment their restaurant idea begins to come to life. Owners are truly the Jacks of all trades and the Kings and Queens of wearing many hats. The goal of this book is to make you more confident in wearing the restaurant accounting hat. It encourages you to know your numbers because numbers define your restaurant's success or failure.

At the beginning of this book, I covered the basic terminology and chart of accounts. I then went on to the fundamentals and logic of setting up a weekly schedule and properly closing the month. I wrapped up by touching on some key terms and simple concepts such as bank feeds, inputting expenses, and cutting checks.

Overall, you now have the tools you need to get started on your own accounting or to better do what you are already doing on your accounting. Remember, the basis of long-term accounting success (and your business success) is to always ask questions. There are plenty of supplementary accounting resources in addition to this book, and you can always reach out to me directly to get more in-depth guidance. Stay hungry, my fellow entrepreneurs.

Here's a toast to your financial success.

STAY UP-TO-DATE

Be on top of the most recent accounting and small business concepts by visiting my blog at **zacweiner.com**. I send out weekly emails with free collateral, resources, and tools to help you better run your business.

ABOUT THE AUTHOR

Zachary Weiner is a full-time business consultant helping small- to medium-sized businesses achieve their financial and operational goals. He specializes in restaurants, hospitality, startups, and real estate from pre-revenue to annual revenue of up to tens of millions of dollars. An entrepreneur and an economist by training, Zachary has written numerous bestselling books and guides that have helped thousands of small business owners and operators better manage their finances. His newest book brings a new and easy-to-understand perspective to the world of restaurant accounting. Zachary currently lives in New York City.

GET IN TOUCH

If you'd like to know when my next book comes out and want to read similar writing every week, sign up at zacweiner.com for my mailing list. Follow me on twitter at @zacweiner and Instagram at @zac_weiner.

Interested in getting some honest and candid feedback about your business finances? Feel free to email me at zac@zacweiner.com or visit the Services section on my website.

If you found anything in this book remotely valuable, there are two ways you could give me a thanks. First, refer this book to a friend who you think will find it beneficial. Second, give me heartfelt review on the web or social media.

Made in the USA
Las Vegas, NV
07 November 2021